THE KITE MAKERS

SIX YEARS OF A CHILD'S WAR - BRITAIN 1939-1945

ANITA SINCLAIR

RICHARD LEE PUBLISHING

Line drawings by Anita Sinclair.

Book design by Richard Lee

Author photo by Vivien Markham

Published by Richard Lee Publishing, Unit 6, 4 Chapel Street South, Maldon 3463 Australia.

Copyright © 2021 Anita Sinclair

ISBN 978-0-909431-17-4

❀ Created with Vellum

To my parents, Win and Wal Baker and all other unsung heroes.

CONTENTS

FOREWORD

They're all dead now; the people I might hurt by writing this: my mother, father, brother. Some cousins, distant or close, must be seventy or eighty years old by now, but most of these will feature only minimally in the telling. Perhaps they themselves write and are willing to reflect on the years of the war – our childhood.

In September 1939 I was not yet three years old. I remember much of that time, due in part to the extreme nature of events. Where scenes are recalled that I may not have personally witnessed, I knew of them. I knew what had happened; I know what was said. I can accurately assign the words to, say, my mother, Winfred May Baker, or to my aunt, Anne Page.

Where I have needed to reconstruct actual events, or to insert dialogue to recreate a scene for the reader, it has been with assured and detailed knowledge of what had occurred. Much dialogue is exactly reported.

This story is true. I have been an artist all my life. I have a vivid visual memory. The images of war I bring to you come through the eyes of a young child. I believe this to be a special perspective.

Now I must Time-travel to relive those six years from 1939 to 1945.

I am eighty-four years old at the time of publishing and not immortal. It's time to do this while my generation is still here. Some of us.

I invite you to enjoy this as a story, but one which is true in all essentials.

CHRONOLOGY

Those readers who remember their childhood (and some don't or claim that they don't) will perhaps be aware that the *date* of an occurrence is not necessarily fixed in the childhood memory. Notable exceptions might be 'that Christmas' or 'that birthday', but even there the year might have to be worked out by the age associated with the event: 'I was seven at the time....'

I have tried to help myself and the reader by reporting the age I had reached at a given time, but frequently found it helpful to consider the year that must have been. I would, at three years old, not have known the numbering of a given year.

Important events marking the commencement and the progress of the war between England, Germany and their allies intruded in stages into my awareness.

Adults shielded much from children (who, they believed, don't understand such things) but we heard the news on the wireless, we listened in determinedly on adult conversation and at the least, got the gist of situations as they arose. This book points to many reasons why I had learned to pay attention.

I had become a close observer.

A person with a more exact knowledge of History may well be able to fault my identification of a year or a month of the war. I have not thought it necessary, or even perhaps honest, to research this information further than I have. I see no value in showing the child I was, nor the adult I have become to be as informed as such exact details might make me appear. Rather, I hope to demonstrate the view of the child in a circumstance which was remarkable, but which the child could compare with no other, thus viewing it all as 'normal'.

I have discovered as I read back over the writing, how frequently I have switched back and forward in time, in one instance speaking as a three year old, in the next, reflecting as an octogenarian; thinking and feeling as a child and in the next paragraph, responding to the memory with adult observations.

Until further notice, I shall regard this as an inevitable aspect of the process of the story telling; the telling of true memories.

PROLOGUE

'I'll give you a ring tomorrow, then.'

They were just back from the dance and talking in whispers. Win had climbed out a window again in her best things and whipped off to the corner where her girlfriend Queenie was waiting.

It was a bit of a walk to the Hammersmith Palais in the new shoes, but worth every bit.

Dad would be furious if he knew, but Harry encouraged her. She knew her brothers all spoiled her, had done so ever since Mum died. That was when she was nineteen. For Heaven's sake, she's twenty-one now – got the 'key of the door', you'd think. But No. Dad was strict. Not with his own goings on, but he knew what happened to girls who were flighty. Well enough: he was one of the things that happened to some of them.

'Mrs. McAllister's not going to be happy if you ring too early, Wally.'

The phone was in the neighbours' house up the street. They had money. He had some sort of special job on the railways. They were pretty good about phone messages, but had an opinion about handsome young sailor boys ringing up young girls.

'Mrs. McAllister's not getting it. I'm giving it to you.'

Oh! He'd already given something to her! Win and Wal had let things go a bit too far. She'd had to tell him. She knew. She knew what had happened to Edie, unmarried when Phyllis came along. All that going to dances at the Palais, all the Charlestons and Modern Waltzes. Dad was right after all. It led to trouble.

Win's 'trouble' came along in the form of a smashing looking sailor who could dance so beautifully, could talk some sweet stuff and make you laugh all the time.

He had been seeing the girls home lately, Queenie to her house first, then Win to a nice shady spot near her place. Queenie had been a bit envious. But not now.

'You'll give me...what? What are you saying, Wally?'

'See you tomorrow.

'I'll give you a ring.'

January 16th 1935.

The Registry Office looked official. The clerk looked official.

Win and Wal had dressed a bit, trying to make the day special. He was in uniform of course, but had had a fresh hair-cut. Win wore a light grey pinstriped two-piece suit with very stylish shoulder pads, a lacy white blouse to look feminine and a corsage pinned to the left lapel. Not real flowers of course, it was mid January and freezing cold. They were violets made out of 'new' bread, soft and malleable, dyed purple, very pretty.

Queenie had made them, so she had a corsage too. You squashed the soft new bread with your finger tips and shaped each petal; then you put them together into flowers. Then the same with the green dyed leaves.

Queenie was good at that sort of thing; she didn't knit, though. Win knitted.

Anne, Win's sister was the other witness for the ceremony,

such as it was. Queenie had not thought of a corsage for her. That was a bit embarrassing.

'Winifred May Martin,' Win informed the Registrar.

'Walter Baker.'

'No middle name, Sir?'

'No, I'm sure I'd know if there was......Sir'.

'That's alright then.' No sense of humour. Not the time for it.

Words said. Papers signed. Done. They were married.

All the horrid decisions were in the past: what to do? How to tell Dad? And Anne? And Harry and everyone. Fred had been better about it. Was that because he was a sailor too and had some idea? He was older than Win and younger than Harry. Anne was the oldest and had to be 'mother' for years now.

Anne knew things. Even how to get out of 'trouble'.

No! That wouldn't do! Wally wouldn't hear of it. It was very risky, Win could get hurt. He got her that 'ring' instead. Three diamonds diagonally across a gold band. Mrs. McAllister's phone was left out of it and they planned a wedding – a marriage ceremony – she wouldn't call it a 'wedding'. She was secretly sad about that: no white dress, no bridesmaids.

But a diamond ring and then a plain gold band, and a room in a basement all to themselves!

Tonight they could roll around in a double bed together with no-one to see or care.

Always together now!

Wal went back to his ship next day.

Win started to make the room nice and shop for 2ply wool for the little 'matinee' jacket and baby layette set she must put together.

Seven months to go.

August 16th 1935.

'Take him away! He's not mine, he's got red hair. I don't want him!'

The midwife was not moved by this. She had experienced many and varied reactions from new mothers at the moment of childbirth.

The unfortunate child had emerged into a small, somewhat bleak basement room – a home birth was quite usual. The father had roamed the streets to escape the screaming that preceded the arrival of the child; the same child that had hurried their marriage. A child now rejected by his mother.

The baby boy was small, but did not need hospital care at six and a quarter pounds. Just love. Like any other baby.

Win was able to breast feed at first, but developed mastitis soon: generally speaking, an unpropitious start to life for a colicky baby with a reluctant set of parents. He was circumcised and Christened Anthony.

Fifteen months later his sister appeared, plump and pretty – a girl. A 'good' baby. Win chose 'Janet' for the baby's name. Wal insisted on 'Anita', a name he had read in a book.

1

DANESBURY ROAD 1939

The house just was.

I can't see the exact house in my mind's eye now, but I believe that I couldn't then either. I didn't need to.

The house had existence as a place, a position in the street, a location that contained my mother. She also had only a general direction at that stage, not a 'look'. She was the thing called Mummy, sometimes Your Mother, the always there, the cause of meals, clothing, bedtime.

At this time in my life I had no particular reason for noticing details about either the house or her.

I know now that Winifred May Baker was pretty and small, with black shiny hair done up in sausage curls on top of her head, one or two falling artfully forward at the front – all very much the vogue. The hair at the back of her head slid smoothly down to turn into a long shining roll round her neck, curving up at the sides behind her ears. She was twenty-seven, thin, vivacious and energetic, efficient, disciplined, fiercely loyal, and fastidious around the house. She was nervous, afraid of physical contact and while strongly attracted to men harboured a deep and secret contempt for them. She spoke very clearly, firmly and knowingly.

These were some of the aspects of my mother that I would be able to notice when later I needed to notice them. At just under three years of age I needed only that she be there, in the house, in Danesbury Road, Feltham, England.

One chilly morning in late Autumn, my mother had given me my breakfast; as usual not negotiating content or quantity but simply placing it in front of me. My meals always simply appeared. No preamble, suddenly, there it is: food; in front of me. Eat it. I know that's what happens next according to my mother.

But I gaze at the bowl. Porridge swimming in milk. The porridge is the creamy sort, not chunky. Its smooth white surface is shiny, its edges have a delicious way of meeting the sea of the milk, its island shapes have set; the sugar crystals sit on top catching the light.

I put my face close taking in the smell of it, focusing and unfocusing my eyes on the sugar granules, playing with the light. If I push the solid shape of the porridge it slides sideways. If I cut a piece out with my spoon the milk slips into the space. The piece I took out makes a new island.

'Do you still want that? Are you going to eat it?' I jumped and came back from my dreaming.

My mother was moving differently this morning. She was working up to something. I had learned to watch her movements: if certain kinds of movement were accompanied by a change of voice I needed to raise my guard.

I lifted my eyes and regarded her carefully. I put a spoonful of food in my mouth but my attention had switched to Mummy, away from eating. The porridge sat tasteless on my tongue as I watched her clean up the rest of the breakfast. She was upset; not with me. She didn't really mind if I ate the porridge or not. Her eyes were moving quickly, alighting on one thing after another, shining a little too brightly. Not seeing.

'Come on Nita, we're going out. Let's get your coat on, it's cold this morning, you'll need your scarf.'

She took my coat in her hands and squatted in front of me. I let her draw the sleeves of my warm coat one after the other up my arms and looked over her face as she buttoned up the double-breasted front and turned down the collar. I already had on my fawn wool leggings and button shoes.

'Where are we going Mummy?' I asked her carefully, quietly, not to add to her nervousness.

'Nowhere much, just up the street. I want to see something. We won't take long.'

It didn't sound too strange, so why were her eyes so bright?

I made myself very still, very un-upsetting, and waited. She had forgotten my scarf. She fetched her grey gabardine raincoat and put it on, threading the flat belt through the loops and slowly tying a knot in front. The sight of her in such a hurry, yet moving as if calmly, carefully, made my tummy feel strange, but the overriding feeling was curiosity: something new was happening, something interesting. If my mother's behaviour was any indication, something very exciting.

It was hard to wait for her to initiate the next move.

I stood quietly, my arms at my sides, my feet together, my 'good girl' persona switched to high. This always got good results. I had an excellent reputation for being a good girl. This was said of me quite regularly – by my mother, our relatives, neighbours and even shopkeepers. My mother (smugly I thought) maintained that you couldn't spoil some children. This was me. This was not my brother, who she was ever diligent not to spoil. He, it seemed, needed plenty of influence in the not spoiling direction and was delivered of this frequently and firmly. I knew that he needed as much improvement according to my mother, as I needed none. This was an odd phenomenon. I was good, he was bad. It had always been so. I was clever, he was silly. I was clean, he wet his bed every night.

These differences were a mystery to me, beyond my understanding, yet they were truths seen daily in all their aspects, resulting in patterns of cause and effect, deeds done, rewards and punishments given. That my brother and I were different could never be doubted. That the rules for one could never be the rules for the other I had always known.

The very fairness with which my mother tried to treat us only made matters worse.

The same naughtiness resulted in the same censure; our mother meted out punishments with exacting fairness, but a smack on the hand or a cross word is received very differently by a child who knows how soon the next one must (justly) occur than the child who gets it so rarely as to not see it as any more than a surprising and temporary aberration. My brother did everything to inspire our mother's wrath and never failed to perceive it as a personal indictment against his character and a measure of her lack of love for him. I had learnt early to 'make a small target' as they say in fencing.

I kept quiet, played the game of parent/child by the rules, stayed out of trouble.

This way I could keep my peace with the world. This way the world maintained peace with me.

So, on this morning late in 1939 I waited patiently, on the outside at least, while my mother located her umbrella and handbag. At last she opened the front door, took my hand and led me out through the front gate, down Danesbury Road past all the neighbours' houses, to where a great space appeared in front of a very odd looking house with whole walls missing and broken windows with blank human faces behind them.

There she and I stood studying our very first bomb crater.

My mother was right, this definitely was different. For a start, I hadn't seen anything as big as this that wasn't a house. This was something.

I was only half aware of my mother, still holding my arm up hanging from her hand. My eyes moved over the scene.

A great hole took up all the space in front of me, its sides were neatly sloped to meet at the bottom making a slight bowl that I could see by leaning over a little. It all made a sort of triangle, though this was not a word I knew then. The sides of the hole were very straight and made two sides of my triangle, and an imaginary line across the top made the third. It was not the same shape as a pudding basin, the closest thing I could imagine like it. I could have slid down the sides in a box it was so smooth – although there seemed to be some bits of junk sticking out here and there. I could hurt myself on those.

A light drizzle of rain blurred the view. Three men in heavy clothing moved in a desultory fashion in and around the crater. Blank grey faces continued to watch from inside the smashed windows. It seemed to me that they were going to get wet with those great black gaping holes in the glass.

'Did the naughty men do that?' I asked my mother eventually.

'Yes,' she said, not looking at me, still held by the implications the scene brought to her.

I thought about this. I had put my question as if referring to the men in the crater. She answered in the same vein. This is my first memory of knowing the evasion in my mother's words and of joining a contract not to expose it. She needed me not to know what had happened. I needed her to be calm about me.

Without directly linking the cause and effect of heavy, sonorous aircraft engine noises in the night, the unexplained loud dull thumps of explosion and the wild looks on the faces of the adults, I felt in my bones the connection between these phenomena and the overnight disappearance of one and a half houses in Danesbury Road, the passivity of the few neighbours standing around in the rain and my mother's sudden need to lie to me.

Where It Began - 1939

I had been born in November 1936 in a tiny workers' cottage in Holly Road Chiswick, immediately outside London. The front door opened onto a very narrow concrete 'area' separated from the pavement by a low brick and cement wall. My only reason for remembering its appearance was the drama I created when my brother, Tony, and cousin Connie had been invited to a children's party and I had not.

The 'good girl' in me succumbed to the demands of the 'neglected, ignored, abandoned' two and a half year old who, like Cinderella, was *not invited.*

Thankfully, my Mother caved in under the unexpected

onslaught and walked me along the row of identical houses to the door of the neighbours' who, again thankfully, let me in. I spent the whole party, not with the other children, who scared me, but on the knee of an indulgent uncle.

Soon, another emotional crisis arose in the same street – indeed, on the street.

It was late 1939. England was at war with Germany. Germany was threatening to use mustard gas on England's cities.

I remember screaming my lungs out as my poor mother tried to put onto my face the latest in Mickey Mouse gas masks. It didn't fool me for one moment, with its stupid round Mickey Mouse ears.

Mickey had a face, not ears stuck on an ugly black rubber thing; he had a nose, not a round hard thing with holes in it. This was really scary. I was stifled by the combined smells of rubber and carbon; the hateful thing was front heavy and cold; I couldn't breath but I could yell all right.

I never wore that gas mask. Many years later, as an experienced sculptor, I would observe the full gas masks in a friend's storage cupboard and tell myself that one day I would put one of them on. I never have.

Few events stood out from the repeat pattern of the days, the routine cycles of seeming calm and sudden action. We children learned the requirements of shelter inasmuch as we could seek it out. Early in the war the public air raid shelters appeared, but not the back yard shelters that followed later.

In Holly Road, we had no basement, but then again, people that had them were often as not trapped in those very basements when their three-storey houses came down.

Days passed in a regular though not reliable routine. A happy change came to me out of no-where.

My mother worked in the Post Office, had done so since she was fourteen and very good at 'speed and accuracy' in Mental Arithmetic. Now the Post was designated an essential service and took her away from the home each day. This turned out well for me, as I was sent off to school with my brother so that I was looked after. I was well under-age, but more than ready to grab this new opportunity that really belonged to the big kids.

Just walking to school was a major privilege; the freedom of going anywhere without adult supervision. The war brought with it many opportunities for early independence. If a child could manage alone or with other children, adults, doting parents included, must release them to do so.

There were few cars on the roads back then and nearly none on our home streets. The streets were narrow and repeated the pattern of Holly Road with monotonous certainty. Cobbled alleyways linked the streets at right-angles. The walk to school was short.

In this wondrous new school environment, my days could be spent at a long low wooden bench shaping fairies out of plasticine and making up stories for them in my head, or holding a slate with a wooden frame around it and drawing a cat or dog or house with white chalk. Or else, with a hard little crayon from a thin cigarette tin, drawing on special coloured paper that the teacher put one page at a time in front of us. These hard crayons came in different colours and had a smell that stayed with me for life. These were not chalks or oil pastels; they were thin and square in section and made a hard sound as you drew. I ignored the other children. They ignored me.

I loved school.

I worried about school when I heard that we were moving out of the Holly Road house to a house in Danesbury Road, Feltham, a bit further away from the centre of London.

I now wonder if this move occurred so that we could be near

Auntie Rose, Daddy's sister. That didn't seem to work out so well. Among other things, my mother refused to drink Auntie Rose's tea because it was served in cracked and dirty cups. She thought I was out of earshot when she said to her sister Anne that 'Rose is rather common.' The word 'common' was weighted with much meaning. Our family was Working Class and Hard Up, but never 'common'.

There was some possibility that Danesbury Road Feltham could be seen to be safer from the now frequent bombing, since it was outside London. The overnight appearance of a bomb crater dispelled that illusion.

'Look what I've got, Mrs. Cooper!' I cried as I rushed into the neighbour's house two doors down.

I held my trophy high. I was desperately excited.

'What is it dear?' Mrs. Cooper recognised the importance of the situation when a very small girl has news.

'A postcard! A postcard from Daddy!' I could hardly speak.

'Let me see, then.' Mrs. Cooper's manners were impeccable.

She sat down, stopped making bread and butter, brushed her hands very clean on her pinny and finally took possession of my treasure. She turned it over; and again. This was a proud moment.

'That's a destroyer dear, isn't it?' she said admiringly. 'Your Daddy's ship, isn't it?'

'Yes, yes, and he's written on the back!' (Quickly, please, turn it over and read it).

"My darling Nita, I'm thinking of you and when I can come home and see you. Be a good girl for Mummy, love, Daddy."

'Well, that's really lovely, isn't it, a postcard just for you. You'll have to put it somewhere safe and keep it. That must be your Daddy's ship on the front.' Mrs. Cooper was inclined to

repeat herself, but I could have kept this conversation going for
hours yet.

'Yes, Daddy's on a destroyer, in the sea. With guns and flags
and everything!'

'Mr. Cooper's in the army, you know. Would you like to see
my picture?'

What a wonderful, magical way to spend half an hour.
Eating slabs of bread spread with butter and sprinkled with
sugar, we studied our pictures over and over, talking ship talk -
flags, funnels and masts and stuff.

Mrs. Cooper knew a thing or two about little girls. I thought
myself very lucky to know someone like her who had butter and
sugar to offer. I never saw any other children at her house, so
that explained I supposed why she had extra rations to share. At
our house we could never be so rash as to squander our sugar on
slices of bread. Our butter ration was always blended half and
half with pale margarine.

Every afternoon about three o'clock I was welcome at Mrs.
Cooper's for bread and butter and sugar. The voluptuous pleasure of it was so intense it embarrassed me. I did my best to
seem relaxed about the business. Little girls, I was told, must not
be greedy. Never was I told this by Mrs. Cooper, my great and
very own friend I had all to myself.

Our house was seldom empty, but just now it was a bit quiet;
my brother was in hospital again with his 'glands.' Every once in
a while he would become unaccountably sick. Glands in his
neck, his groin, under his arms would swell up and once again
he would be off to hospital for a spell.

My father was 'at sea.' This explained, apparently, his sudden
disappearance from my life.

Such a handsome man. Dad was dark, the black Span-
ish/Irish hair fine and straight on both his head and his beautifully shaped eyebrows. His mouth was full and smiling, his teeth

quite perfect in shape and whiteness, his eyes the clearest of blues. He had a perfectly straight nose and I adored him. He was quite the love of my life for all of my three years. My affection was returned in such degree that I felt a confusing jealousy coming from my mother at times, in a word or a look. This was so amazing to me that I thought it couldn't be as it seemed. As time went by, it came clearer to me.

As it was, my beloved Daddy had gone away. Just, suddenly, was not there. Gone. Nobody said where or why.

No doubt my mother was upset enough on her own account. She loved him very unreservedly. Certainly she would not have produced me had she not adored him. After Tony my brother was born, she was told firmly not to become pregnant again, not to have any more children. My existence at all was due to her inability to say No to her man.

It never occurred to me to think that she also had lost him, had lost her mate, her helper, her friend; was alone at twenty-seven with two small children to care for. And a war.

She had photographs of my father in albums and in frames on the sideboard.

There was a very manly looking one of him on a cliff at Land's End, in shorts with his chest bare and his hair blowing in the wind. He was not a large man, but he was well made, with a deep, high pigeon-shaped breast. His skin inclined to honey-brown when tanned. He was not muscular but rather strong. I thought him very heroic looking in that photograph.

I didn't know Mrs. Cooper's husband, or anyone else's for that matter, other than my uncles. The men were all going, either to sea or into the army. Not so many into the air force.

The old chaps in the Home Guard moved somewhere on the outside edge of my world. I knew they were there, somewhere. The Air Raid Wardens came only rarely to check our blackout curtains so that not a chink of light would show to guide the German bombers to us.

· · ·

Mrs. Cooper had an Air Raid shelter in her back garden before we got ours. The standard Anderson shelter, half underground, was made with curved pieces of corrugated iron, creating a rounded roof-and-wall arrangement rising out from an earthen floor. A door at one end provided access. From the outside all that showed was soil heaped up over the curved iron and covered with grass. The belief was that only a 'direct hit' would demolish such a shelter. In this instance, the occupants didn't stand a chance.

We would all snuggle inside the small shelter with blankets wrapped around and a half-lemon sweetened with more of Mrs. Cooper's sugar to suck, presumably to keep us busy. I had paper to draw on if it wasn't too late, it usually was. Our mother was inclined to settle Tony and me down to sleep as early as she could.

Next evening, Mrs. Cooper would have lemons and sugar ready to give us again.

It was in Danesbury Road that we viewed our first bomb crater, so any idea my mother might have had of Feltham being safer than Holly Road, Chiswick was swiftly modified.

My Mother

I took my mother for granted. She was the half-ignored essential centre of my life. She had always been there, a constant; trusted within the usual limits of trust with which a child might surround a parent. Clearly my safety and health was to her, paramount.

I knew I represented something to her, something like a mirror, or no, a kind of second, luckier version of herself.

Like many parents before and after her, she was sure her child was getting a much better deal than she had ever got. She called me 'Lady Jane' or 'Lady Jane Grey' at times, cutting me down to size it seems, by telling me I behaved as if I were used to servants waiting on me hand and foot. I was barely three now, and couldn't see the problem. However, I understood her tone.

Still she was my life preserver, carer, loving parent. She truly cared; she always did her very best. The fact that temperamentally we were chalk and cheese to each other didn't matter so much. I knew she would die for me.

In a general sort of way she was a heroine to me: my guard, my own special safe person. The day would come when she would demonstrate this by pulling off an amazing rescue, flaunting her opinion against the wishes of the government and against the more conservative views of her friends. Her husband's opinion didn't come into it; he was in the North Sea at the time and had problems of his own.

Evacuation Plans

Neville Chamberlain had finally declared war on Germany, after disgraceful attempts to negotiate an 'honourable peace' with a man quite devoid of honour.

In no time flat Hitler was dropping bombs on England's green and pleasant lands, but more particularly, over her densely populated cities, with no discrimination at all as to military targets. His goal over a long period was to break the spirit of the people.

One thousand bombers per day were crossing the channel, dumping their bombs and returning to Germany for more.

Britain knew that metal for armaments was not the only thing she would run out of soon. Soon there might be no next generation of Britons. One thousand bombers a day can place a lot of incendiary bombs where children might reasonably be. Where then, will be the families of the future if the children of the present are all wiped out?

The British government had anticipated such a possibility for more than six years, having drawn certain conclusions from World War 1. How can it be that some men saw this coming for so long to the degree that they made plans as early as 1931 for massive evacuations out of the cities, yet at a time when Hitler was helping himself to bits of Czechoslovakia others of them could sustain a fantasy of peace?

Organisers of the evacuation were keen to set up an orderly withdrawal from the east coast cities. Better the dam be opened methodically by themselves than that it burst all in a rush.

In the event of war, the poor, it was thought, would surely panic. The wealthy could make their own way, but a system had to be put in place to regulate the retreat of the poor from the path of the bombing. This was being organised in one room as it were, whilst in another Chamberlain was relishing his success with Hitler and basking in the warmth of 'peace in our time.'

The first evacuation trains left the cities on September 1st 1939, two days before Chamberlain faced reality and declared war on Germany on September 3rd.

I would turn three on November 14th. Tony had turned four in August.

My mother faced an impossible situation. Later, in the 1990s, she seemed to think that one ticket in Tatts could stand a chance to win her a fortune. In early 1940 she wasn't happy about similar odds maybe sparing her children.

The government had the evacuation under way.

My brother Tony no sooner got well enough to come out of hospital than he was packed onto a train with his little cardboard suit case, his name label on his coat and his cardboard gas mask box on a string around his neck.

He had joined proudly in the school rehearsals for the great exodus. Now he was ready to see the world!

The evacuation trains headed west stopping at small towns along the way, off-loading a few kids each time and obliging the locals to take them into their homes. Tony ended up in a house outside Penzance in Cornwall, with about fourteen other city bred souls.

Parents had not been allowed to accompany children - not even onto the train station platform itself. Their last sighting of their various heirs, treasures and liabilities was at a distance, through a train carriage window, pressed grotesquely against the glass or stuck bravely smiling through an open space in the door.

The children wore moods ranging from anticipation through grief to anesthesia. For some it had the feel of their own private Odyssey and for others it might only not be worse than they had seen day by day for as long as they could remember.

The saddest of a sorry lot were the ones who didn't know what was happening and were altogether too young to leave their mothers.

A very few mothers had been permitted to accompany their babies in the evacuation, but this only occurred where the child was an infant in arms. Tony was too old to qualify; his mother must stay in London.

Apparently another loophole existed from the general rule: if a woman was willing to take with her a number of children not her own, she was able to evacuate together with them all.

The house near Penzance had two such women supervising their own two children and twelve others.

The house itself did not of course belong to them. Its owners had been obliged by the government to give it over to the evacuation program. Many country properties were taken over in this way to 'aid the war effort.' Houses that sat empty for one reason or another were claimed by local councils and used for the evacuees. Other homes with local families living in them took in the quota of city children assigned to them.

This house was something of a plain country dwelling, being grander than a cottage, but not grand in concept or design and certainly no Stately Home.

The evacuees came from all levels of society but mostly the poorer sections, it being possible for those families with money to remove themselves from the east coast areas and not depend upon the government program.

The two women who moved into this particular house had a situation now that offered them: income from the government for the upkeep of the children they took in, furniture and bedding found for them by the local council and a house they could depend upon for the duration of the war.

They soon developed the habit of regular contact with parents for additional monies and improved their own immediate circumstances by budgeting – a euphemism for skimping on food supplies for the children in their care. Rationing was in place now, but given their new circumstance, they could see to it that they and their own two children would not do without.

This was the destination towards which Tony traveled, with his dreams of high adventure only slightly dented by the length of the journey.

My mother and I were alone again.

Every evening she cleaned up after an early meal, then sat on the back doorstep waiting for the air raid siren. If it was raining she rearranged the damp clothes on the clotheshorse, polished our shoes, folded linen, looked for something else to do and waited for the air raid siren.

Every night we checked the searchlights and barrage balloons in the sky, and in the company of the siren's wail climbed down into one shelter or another, where we lay listening, becoming lifetime experts on exact plane sounds:

'That's theirs, that's Jerry.'

'That's ours.'

Every morning London examined its scars and collected its dead.

My mother's resolve cracked. She had thought me too young to send away. Now, I suppose, she thought me too young to die.

The evacuation trains as such had stopped, so she packed me

up, dressed me in my sensible clothes, put my toys in my case and bundled us both into a railway carriage for Cornwall to join my brother. She was to leave us together and return home.

Perhaps she imagined that my brother, a full fifteen months older than I, would be able to take care of his little sister.

Poor lady; her son was not yet five years old.

2

CORNWALL 1940

Cornwall changed my life.

At three and a bit years of age I went through an initiation that would set my eyes, hands, feet, heart and mind on the path they would follow for life.

In a live-or-die situation I chose to live.

In a world where I had nothing and no-one I started to build a new inner world, unassailable from the outside, a world in which I could turn private fantasy into physical reality. At three and a bit years of age I became an artist.

Cornwall severed forever the close bond I had with my mother. That which had always been there was gone. The one human being that was permanent to me, never absent, was gone.

This followed closely enough on the disappearance of my father who, while adored beyond measure, had yet never ministered as my mother did to my daily needs, dressing me, washing me, making all my decisions for me.

Nothing had prepared me for the loss of this.

Not a sock had I ever put on by myself. The little quilted cotton 'liberty bodice' I wore tight around my chest had a long row of tiny metal buttons to close it; A long row of tiny pearl buttons closed the centre back. I might as well have been sewn into it for all the hope I had of removing or replacing it. I had never in my life brushed my own hair.

A generation later when I was a parent, I saw to it that my children could handle every aspect of their daily dressing, grooming, toilet and feeding needs.

Never could I bear to imagine a child of mine rendered totally helpless and incompetent by my absence.

'Two please, one adult return and one half one way. Thank you.'

The most wonderful aspect of train travel was for me the smells. The impossibly huge train station with its clocks, its ticket boxes and its notices was redolent with fumes. The breakfast smells coming from the tea room, the biting smoke from the exhausts of the traffic outside in the street and the heady machine oil smells from everywhere.

The platform itself was a mass of steam. I had views in all directions of the middle and lower regions of adult bodies crowding round, blocking, then revealing, then crowding in again.

My mother hurried us into a carriage, found a compartment and installed me in a window seat, my small cardboard suitcase in the overhead rack and herself opposite me.

She was speaking in a managing sort of way with a particular cheerfulness that made me wonder.

'See that man with the flag, Nita? He tells the train when to go. Oh, look at that poor lady with all the luggage, oops! It's all right, the porter's going to help her. That pram shouldn't be so close to the edge of the platform. Have you got both your gloves? I can only see one. Look at that soldier. He must have been home on leave. I wonder if he's got a little girl?'

She was running on her own energy. I said not a word and this didn't slow her down one bit.

'See, that's his kit bag; that's instead of a case. Daddy's got one of those but his is black, or is it very dark blue? – look, there's a sailor!'

There was a bunch of them actually, with some girls, big, big girls that were not the same as mummies somehow. One of them was sniffling into a handkerchief and rolling her eyes stupidly at a quite uninterested sailor boy. They were juggling cigarettes, kit bags, girls hands and kisses, and cramming one by one up the steps and into our carriage door. As they passed our compartment they all talked at once and loudly, the smoke from their Craven A's floating in through our door.

'They must have only just joined up,' my mother observed, 'Their collars are still very dark.' This enigmatic remark faded into and out of my consciousness. I craned my head to look in the direction of the platform behind me. Maybe we'll be going soon. People are starting to rush around and shout at each other.

I was stirred by a great sense of adventure. Just like in my story books we were off to strange lands!

So many things to see. How important we were, getting on a train!

'I need to have a wee, mummy.'

The train started up with a great lurch.

We arrived at the house in Penzance to find two women and two children alone. My brother was out somewhere with the other children.

My mother had only one hour before she had to return by train to London. Well, that's what she said. She seemed as if she wanted to go somewhere anyway. I didn't really pay attention, there was so much else to think about.

I stared at the two children.

Mummy had lots of things to talk about with the strange ladies.

I was used to hanging around adults while they were talking

and had no inclination at all to join in. I was busy digesting what I could see of this new place.

I had always had the habit of playing my eyes over anything and everything. Just as a sightless child seeks out sound and motion constantly, often rocking, often chatting on and on, to keep their sense of placement in their environment, I had instead always run my eyes around, eating up visual stimuli. If indeed we are made differently, my difference had always been this visual recording, operating at a subconscious level all the time, conscious a lot of the time. Without my necessarily meaning to, I was recording scenes and people in detail and was later assailed by vivid visual memories whenever I thought back, for better or for worse. These I could draw and paint from the moving pictures in my mind. They could easily blot out the real world for whole slabs of time. Quite horribly when they appeared as nightmares.

Here in this house there was a sense of darkness, of obscurity.

A half-hearted light filtered in through the grubby multi-paned window into a dim rectangular room from which any object of sentiment must have been removed by the vacating owners. This room had nothing entertaining to offer the eyes of a little girl: nothing to distract her from the fact of a very anxious mother trying to make civil conversation with strangers.

The room was furnished yet barren; occupied yet lonely. I waited.

'I have to go now, Nita.'

My mother suddenly turned to me. She dropped to her haunches in front of me and grasped me tightly in a clumsy hug.

'Be a good girl for the Aunties, won't you?' she added as an afterthought.

With my history she probably wouldn't expect me to do much else.

'Mummy, are you going somewhere? Aren't I coming? Where are you going? When are you coming back?'

I was starting to get the sense of what was happening here.

'Oh, soon dear, soon, as soon as I can. Mummy will write letters to you. Be a good girl. Don't cry.'

This with her own eyes getting wet.

A rushed kiss, a squeeze of the hand, and she was out the door.

The Toys

I was in a bleak room with my little suitcase and my gas mask box, looking at two women and two children, a boy of nine, a girl of twelve. I waited.

I watched the girl sidle across to the window and rub a viewing hole in the grime. Her frock didn't fit her very well, it looked like it belonged to someone bigger. Mummy used to fix my frocks for me if they were too big when we got them. My cousin Connie was a lot bigger, so when she finished with a frock and handed it on, Mummy got out her sewing machine with the fold-down handle and made it to fit me.

This girl was skinny like Connie, but taller too. Her face looked dangerous somehow; her mouth was shut tight and her chin stuck out. She didn't look at me once.

She watched out the window as my mother walked out of sight.

'Go and play with Nita, you two,' said one of the women, 'Take her outside or something.'

The girl turned and glared at her mother and promptly left the room; the boy made no response at all. He and I at least knew of the void that separated us and were happy to let the length of the room fail to fill it.

He had a face like a suet pudding, pasty, lumpy and round. His currant eyes were stupid and motionless as he stared at me. He was bigger than me, bigger than my brother too. His arms had to go in a kind of a bend to hang down beside his body. His clothes looked lumpy like his face. You'd think he'd pull his socks up. His knees were grubby in his grey short trousers and his shoes tipped outward at an angle. His fingers were wiggling all the time as if they were doing all his thinking.

The lady who spoke was probably his mother, although I never did work that one out for certain; but she had that same shapeless look, with the wrong bit of her body doing the fidgeting. Her elbows jerked in and out as she moved as if to keep her wound up. Her face was pink, squarish and cross-looking; her hair was shorter than my mother's and in a terrible mess. Her mouth moved even when she wasn't saying anything.

She scowled at the boy and made impatient clucking noises as she jerked quickly towards me, picking up my little suitcase and thumping it aggressively onto a chair. To my horror she opened it and started to inspect my worldly possessions.

My mother had fussed over the choice of articles and packed them in with great care, taking them out and replacing them, trying ever better ways to fit more things in. The government had provided lists of requirements for evacuees so that everyone knew what basic clothing and accessories must be taken. In addition to these, my mother had squeezed in such favourite toys and story books as she imagined might sustain me through the weeks, months or years to come.

I had watched her packing with her strange combination of determination and misery, overlaid with what was supposed to pass as cheerful encouragement. In went my pale blue teddy, loved to a state of hairlessness – my favourite and greatest comfort – first! Second, my book of animal stories. In quick succession a rag doll with a sewn-on face, a little plain paper note pad from the Post Office, two short yellow-coloured pencils, sharpened, two more soft toys: a white bunny and a black golly. All these had been pressed in neatly with my changes of underwear, two nighties, a dressing-gown, slippers, socks and toilet things. My gas mask box was separate.

Now all my things were flung over a shoulder, draped over a chair-back or lying in heaps on the floor.

The boy John wandered over to better see what was going on. The other 'Auntie' plonked herself down, still at the far end of the room, watching without interest the decimation of my property.

I put my hands behind my back so that they would not reach out.

Suddenly the door flew open and the room was filled, first by cold air, then by the noise and scramble of many children.

'Shut that bloody door,' yelled the nearest Auntie.

Coats were removed, shoes wiped, scarves and mittens dumped on a bench next to the door.

'Sit down will you! There's someone new.'

I had a healthy terror of older children, since my brother and cousins were all older than I and the significant two, my brother and my cousin Connie, were inclined to entertain themselves by baiting me, which for them demonstrated that they were smarter.

My brother had entered the room with the other children, but this made little difference to me, I was rather indifferent to him.

All too many of the children in front of my eyes were older than I was; they moved back and made a space between us, some even sitting down as instructed, all the better to inspect the new element in their lives. They had been in Penzance for a few weeks now, knew the lay of the land and were just beginning to feel knowledgeable about a place which, when first sighted, had shocked them with its complete lack of similarity to London.

If one is used to seeing a horizon, it comes as no surprise. If one has many times seen stars in their profusion brightening the night sky, one ceases to see them soon. These children had previously seen no further than a brick wall with an aged Victorian tenement beyond. Their sky had held no surprises, being uniformly pale grey until the arrival of fat barrage balloons and angling searchlights which had become in their turn commonplace, accepted as symbols of 'home' and now sadly missed. To them the night sky of Cornwall was a surprising thing, magical and beautiful, but not part of 'home.'

This was their new territory then, claimed only weeks before and held with the uneasy knowledge of possible change, to be brought about not by themselves, but by unconnected outside others. These children were embattled, and as such not about to concede an inch of ground that was not wrested from them. No, not even to one abandoned three-year-old girl.

'What's her name, Auntie Jean?' I didn't see where the question came from.

'Why didn't she come before? When we came?' Suspicion arises out of the most trivial doings.

'Sit down, the lot of you. Get your things off the floor Mary, what have I told you?

'Nita, come and sit here next to me.'

I was on automatic now and moved to the chair on the left of the Auntie Jean lady. My eyes took in the room, lined around its walls now with seated children, all of them staring at me still. I felt very tired and didn't know what to do. My mother would usually notice and fix me up with food and bed.

'This is Nita Baker; she's going to stay here now. With us.'

Here it was then, the sentence; spelt out by an indifferent arbiter before a jury of my peers.

Things could not be worse.

Auntie Jean pointed around the group putting names to faces. Not one of these registered on my brain; however, the pale passive masks against the dark of the walls were imprinted forever, and lived on together in my mind as symbols of alienation and dread.

It seemed suddenly that Auntie Jean was stricken with an idea that would resolve all social difficulties and provide everyone with a much-desired alternate focus of attention.

Into my suitcase she plunged and came up with two of my toys.

'There!' she announced triumphantly, handing my bunny and my golly to two of the children.

'Nita can share these with you,' she added, passing out my little drawing pad and pencils.

But she'll leave me my teddy, I thought, seconds before it and my rag doll were passed into eager, grasping hands.

My toys, my friends, my only things, had been taken from me as an act of generosity and sharing; given away by someone I didn't know to others equally foreign.

My mother was gone. I was in Penzance. These were the people. I was to stay here with them.

Something inside me closed over.

As soon as the words, 'Things could not be worse', are uttered, things all too frequently get much worse.

Some days after my arrival in Cornwall we children were sent out for a walk. This was an interesting decision on the part of the Aunties. Penzance, of pirate fame, notorious for its smugglers' inlets and caves, is also known for its violence of sea and gale. None-the-less, to fill an idle Sunday, fifteen city bred children were let loose unsupervised on the pitiless Cornish coast.

At least it got us out of the house.

Penzance is positioned almost on the point of Land's End at the extreme south-western tip of England, tucked into Mount's Bay. It might be possible to describe it as having more protection than St. Just or St. Ives, that were situated northward on the other side of the peninsular, but taken the behaviour of the winds and currents around there, I would think that the Phoenicians of the past and the fishermen of the present would have no justification for dropping their guard at all as they approached these battered and ragged cliffs.

In January freezing Westerly winds circle the Arctic Ocean before sweeping over the Atlantic and cutting up under Ireland and Cornwall. In July a kinder, warmer battering comes over and around from Florida.

On this September day the weather permitted an invigorating walk, while not conceding too much to warmth or to relaxation.

The wind belted our little group energetically from the right as we headed across the open grassland towards the cliffs. I tended not to listen to conversations not directed specifically at me, so I don't know if we were given instructions for or against the sea as a destination. At any rate, Auntie Jean tended to give orders with the tone of one who automatically expects them to produce an opposite result from the one she was asking for. She was too lazy to follow-up any statement she made – unless driven to a simple physical reflex which, while painful for the recipient, did not require a lot of decision making or resolution from herself.

So, off in the direction that promised the most stimulation marched our little band.

As was my usual practice, I lagged behind. This was not only the result of having shorter legs; it really was the easiest way to stay away from other children. They felt better being faster and more effective, I felt better letting them.

Word had it that I was a pretty child: round faced, with very fair hair and curls all over my head, built like a cupid with the standard chubby knees and rosy cheeks. In addition, I was well behaved to the point of total submission.

For these reasons adults took to me. For that reason other children conspired to tip the balance.

Out of sight of the women running the evacuation house, the older children would let me know my place. The approval of the so-called Aunties was no great prize either; it meant only that I would occasionally be pointed out to defaulting nose-wipers, hand washers or shoe scrapers as the standard to which they might aspire. This was a heavy load with no way to shift it except by doing things that, while lumping me in with my peers, would get me in strife with the greatest, most terrifying powers in the house.

I continued to be as good as I could be for the adults, while trying against all odds to fit in with the older children.

Our Sunday morning expeditionary force marched on around a tumble of low gorse, itself struggling for order and attaining it only by leaning away from the west. Now the wind pushed me hard from behind so that I had to do some fancy footwork to stay upright. My hair was flattened forward at the back and tickling around my cheeks at the front. The howling voice of the wind drove everything but its own opinion from my ears; my coat seemed to be collaborating with the gale to drag me forward, and the land began to slope down.

The same circumstances were working on the others ahead of me. They clustered indecisively on the sketchy path.

The air around us was wet now from fine light droplets of sea spray.

A mist floated between me and the rest.

I was well apart from them. I breathed in deeply.

I stood still, swaying like a drunkard, but drunk only on the effect of the massive assault to my senses of biting cold, driving wind and the salt, seaweed fragrance of the roaring incoming tide. For myself, I was alone. Nothing existed but sensation. A seagull cried desolately above somewhere trailing its tragic story on the highest airflow, fading out and sadly wailing in. I closed my eyes and lost myself to sensation. I was alone and in Paradise.

'Nita! Come on! Nita, wake up and come on, you're holding us up! You always hold us up.

'Come ON will you!'

It was the skinny girl, the daughter of Auntie Jean, called Jean by the same instinct for dynasty that named the lumpy boy 'John' after his father. It was an era of 'Johns' and 'Jeans.'

'Don't make me come and get you.' She sounded like her mother. I hurried to catch up.

The children were lined up contemplating the view over the edge of the cliff.

My Paradise faded as I paid attention to them.

'There could be a pyrits cave darn there.' Douglas was leaning right over.

They were of school age and had been read books never to be found in their homes. With the help of their teachers, Robert Louis Stevenson had made his mark.

'I kin see a cave!' Douglas danced and pointed to the left, saving himself by a narrow margin as the others pushed in.

His sister Sheila was skeptical: 'No you kin not, liar. You kin not see anyfing. There weren't any pirates. Liar, liar, liar.'

Time had to be spent now on the evidence for the defence. Nobody else cared about Douglas's reputation but they were biased in favour of a cave finding, so preferred him to be right.

'We kin go and farnd art anyhow. Even if THAT ain't a cave, I bet there is PLENTY a caves ararnd. I bet there is 'UNDREDS a caves rarnd 'ere.' Douglas was sticking to his guns.

I started to pay attention properly.

It was a long way down. The tide was in and smashing against the base of the cliff, boiling on the pitted rocks that were scattered randomly where they had fallen as they gave up the fight to hold a place on the cliff wall.

I didn't want to get my shoes wet.

I looked to see where Tony was and saw him in the thick of the group around Douglas. Pirates, Caves and the entirely possible Treasure were pulling him along. No good hoping for escape there. I couldn't walk off on my own and no-one else seemed to want to go.

Douglas was looking for a way over the edge. 'Darn this way. Darn 'ere ev'ryone!'

He was our leader now and the rest of us moved like cattle to follow, bumping, veering off, recovering, then joining in the line as it slithered and scrambled over from scrubby grass to gravelly rock face.

I hung on to the side of the cliff as the crowd shoved past me; dreams of unlikely wealth carrying the more gullible along, fantasies of falling and breaking on the rocks gluing me to the spot.

'I farnd a parf!', yelled Douglas against the howling gale.

He was a tough looking boy, rough from the streets of Pimlico, easily transferring the confidence in his own leadership from there where he knew the territory, to this new terrain which he knew not at all.

His 'parf' was a narrow ledge. If smugglers had ever used it they would definitely not have had the elbow room to carry their loot. We were single file now by absolute necessity. I slid down on my bottom at the back of the line. I knew I would be in big trouble when the Aunties saw my clothes. I was getting quite frightened.

The pack, on the other hand, were full of their high adventure.

'The path ends ere. Stop everyone, we'll ave to go back.' Jean was second in line and old enough to be cautious.

'No it don't. There's anuvver parf starts after this bit of a jump.'

Douglas defended his leadership. One sign of weakness and a girl might take over. Unthinkable.

He tensed his muscles and leapt, landing easily on the other ledge. Jean had a problem. Either she left him there on his own and took over the group, which might anyway elect to follow Douglas, or she risked the jump for herself and the others. Nobody had told her she was in charge of us, but she knew as sure as the strap on the wall that she'd better not go home short of anyone.

'Alright. You make sure and catch'em when they jump. I'll hold'em at this end.'

We were getting wet standing there, and it was really cold now. The bigger kids moved up a bit and Jean got Richard ready for his jump. Over he went.

'That's one.' Somebody with a sense of order was counting.

'Two.' Sheila joined her brother on the other side.

'Three.' 'And Four!' One by one the children jumped. They pushed past Douglas to make a new line on the other end. 'Ten.' It didn't look so hard after all. Tony was lined up, with Jean holding the end of his coat and Douglas ready to catch him.

He looked like he wasn't going to jump for a minute, then off he went. Douglas got him by his waist and swung him onto the path behind him. 'Eleven.'

I could see Tony's face, it was white and shiny.

'The little kids won't be able to reach, Douglas. P'raps I'd better take them back.'

Good, this was a promising trend.

'We cain't split up naow,' cried Douglas, somehow sensing that captains kept the company together.

'I'll come an' carry 'em over.' He jumped.

No. No! Can't I stay here. I really want to stay here.

Douglas picked up the boy in front of me and jumped. They made it. He turned to leap back again.

Suddenly Jean had hold of me. She lifted me up like a baby in arms and got ready to jump. Well, she's a big girl, I thought. She's bigger than Douglas. It must be alright, she's big.

She made as if to jump, then dropped her arms suddenly over the gap. The waves below me roared and raged against the boulders, breaking into white grasping claws as they reached up to grab me.

She dropped me again and caught me. I was nearly dead with fear. I could hear her laughter over the wind and surf.

She hauled me up, shoving her face into mine as she put me back on the ledge. She had evened the score. I might be pretty or I might be a good girl in her mother's eyes, but what was I now? Little. Little enough for her to fix up.

We got back to the house by nightfall, safe in body and changed forever in spirit.

I had learned not to trust blindly that day and to not confuse my general public acceptance with universal goodwill.

I met hatred that afternoon. It was given to me freely. I took it and tucked it away for later study.

I lay in bed with my eyes closed.

The girls on either side of me were asleep; we were four of us in a double bed and another four were sharing troubled slumbers in the double bed across the room.

I breathed in; the room smelt of bodies washed with 'Lifebuoy' and the sick of the redheaded girl called Doreen. Aunty Jean had cleaned her up. I hope I don't ever be sick. In the night Doreen would wet the bed again.

I screwed my eyes tighter and pushed the bed covers into my nose.

What was it about the cliff? Not after, before. What was it that was lovely before I caught up with the others?

There was a seagull. And wind; the wind was everywhere: inside my head, around my ears, flying, pushing, singing. And the seagull flew with it, up, up above everything. The sea; remember the sea. Get the sea into it. I can make the smell of the sea come back, and the sound, the roaring and crashing. The wind, the sea, the spray on my face, the cry of the bird; I can bring it all back. I can feel it, smell it, see it, taste it. I can fill my whole body and mind with the picture. A whole terrible, wonderful, feeling picture that nothing else can get into.

My eyes produced tears, which squeezed and rolled down my cheeks, one each side down to the pillow. I wiped my face with the sheet.

The seagull floating. I'm a fairy on his back. I'm a fairy like Tinker Bell and I'm riding on the seagull way up high in the sky. I've got those fine floaty clothes on, flying behind me, and wings like loops of soap bubble they're so thin and shiny. I'm thin and shiny. It's morning and the sun is coming up, everything glows orange like in a picture. I can see down to the ground over the wing of my seagull. There are fields like in Puss In Boots and little cottages with flowers and vegetable gardens. Somebody is driving a cow through a gate. Jack-and-the-Beanstalk had a cow. My seagull is heading for the sea. I've got reins to steer him so we won't go too far out – but maybe we will; maybe we can fly to China; China always sounded wonderful, or to a magic cave like Aladdin! With my seagull I can go anywhere I like. I think he can be called Walter, after my Daddy.

My eyes relaxed, flickered and softened. I succumbed to the gentle persistent call of sleep.

The Kite Makers

The house stood stark and square against the sky, as plain as a child's drawing; white paint-washed and weathered stone walls below, grey slate-tiled roof above. Two chimneys. Three windows up, two down, a central door. Absolutely nothing to draw a visitor in. Blankness on the face of the house and the flat area of yard around it. I spent very little time in studying it, yet I knew its shape and features far more clearly than I did the house in Danesbury Road. That, I could not conjure up at all.

Since my arrival in Cornwall my senses had sharpened. I had been offered several reasons for taking note of my surroundings, several reasons for paying attention to others.

Here, it was necessary to be observant, to anticipate events. Knowing exactly where people and things were positioned was taking up more of my attention than ever before. This was not to suggest that I became more outgoing: I became an observer, a watcher, with a space between myself and others that might not be crossed.

Deep inside myself I felt safe. From there I watched the world.

Things could be studied closely. Inanimate objects around me had patterns, shapes to admire, shades of colour, texture, smell. Sometimes there were insects. My eyes could focus right in and I could see them as if theirs were the real-sized world and mine some outer world thing. I could imagine them thinking, working, having ideas. In my stories about them, they were having great fun!

Outside in the yard, away from the house, I was able to be quite alone. I squatted down on my heels, ready to study my own private universe.

Today was a good day, the children were all at school, except for Tony who had developed sores all over his legs; he was upstairs, I could see him at the window. Now he's gone.

I turned my eyes from the house to the ground. There were rocks, dust and some small scatterings of rubbish here and there.

I looked across the yard to the dry-stone wall. Beyond it I could see only grey sky and the tops of some unhappy looking shrubs. There was a great silence like a sound over everything.

I ran my hand over the gravel and dust. A spot of colour caught my eye, a flash that interrupted the monotonous biscuit sameness around me. I peered closer with the intensity of a chicken studying a bug. A piece of wool, four inches long. Red! I turned around and swept my eyes in an arc. More wool, short pieces, different colours!

Treasure is relative. In a morning totally barren of activity or opportunity for work, a few scraps of wool can represent an abundance of creative possibility. I tied two pieces together.

In my mind appeared an image of my father, seated at his workbench with my brother on one side, myself on the other.

He made magic with string and cord, his years in the navy apparent in the deftness with which he tied intriguing and attractive knots, each one said by him to serve a different and distinct purpose. His fingers were tapered, business-like and very flat at the tips. They obeyed him most precisely. Over-and-under; through; pull; and a beautiful, useful knot was made.

My father gave a strange name to each knot and described the use to which it would be put on board ship. Names like Sheep-shank and Half-hitch stayed in my mind, along with the image of the knot itself. On one occasion he created the spectacular Turk's Head knot in thin leather strips for the end of a neighbour's umbrella handle.

With cord, slats of wood and white cotton cloth, one day he built a kite.

First, a cross was created with two thin slats. One arm of the cross was left much longer than the other three. The cloth was cut and sewn – my father could sew, darn socks and embroider; no idle hours were tolerated when many men were crowded together in His Majesty's ships. Wal had been in the Merchant Navy since he was seventeen. My mother had married a sailor.

Cloth was stretched and secured across the back of the light wooden cross. Linen thread was taken from point to point around the very tips of all the arms, a couple of looser lengths spanned the front and now we three had an article that could fly at the end of a very long cord, way up in the air, far, far, above us.

Before we could test our kite, Daddy had to make a tail, to act as a sort of steadying influence behind. This was made by tying twisted bits of paper along a length of cord. They looked a bit like butterflies.

For the fun of it we painted a face on the white cloth, and

you could see it smiling at you from the sky as if it was having a very good time up there.

I viewed that memory like a loved movie.

A kite! My own kite! I can make one myself!

I only knew one kind of knot – the Granny. My fingers, like the rest of me, were three and a half years old, but I had them under fair control. I took my collection of coloured wools and tied them end-to-end. This took some time, of which I had plenty in that cold Cornish garden.

I needed a kite on the end of my string now. No wood strips in sight; no cotton fabric. I had to think of something else.

A piece of white paper caught my eye. It wasn't much to look at, but I was committed to pretending now. I smoothed it a bit, selected a corner and tied my length of knotted wools to it.

A kite!

I controlled the wind. Out there in that empty landscape I sent my perfect kite up into the sky, running, running with it, holding it high, laughing, calling, rejoicing.

This is my first memory of using my hands to make something; not merely to build but to create an escape from a miserable and inadequate world. Through my little paper and wool kite, I could rise up and fly swiftly and joyously across the broad bright sky.

The days that passed with waking and sleeping, washing and eating, held only such pleasures as my mind could create. My whole mental energy went into searching out the odd, the interesting, the new. Whilst my thoughts were kept busy with these, my feelings could be held down. When I busied myself with explorations and distractions I was not tempted to join the other children in their chosen pursuits.

The Wind Changes

'Nita, Nita!' the wind carried the seagull's voice to me, sounding so much like my name.

I was squatting down out in the far reaches of the farmhouse yard. Nothing grew there. The ground under my shoes was as hard as rock and strewn with rough sand-coloured pebbles. I touched a stone; it was kind of lumpy.

'Neeetaaa.'

I dropped my head backwards so that I could see straight up to the sky. The clouds were low; the seagull was stock still in the air, sitting on a wind pocket, its pleading, appealing, sad-happy voice calling me.

I spent a moment absorbing the peculiar taste of the sea air as it entered my nose and throat. This was Cornwall for me. Not the two 'Aunties' in the house, not the hard-faced children they kept as guests, not my brother, somewhere out of sight. No, Cornwall was seagull's cry; biting, flavourful air, damp and delicious; wind, bare rocky ground and space as far as I could see. The sky was endless, the green grass flats beyond the yard limits continuing uninterrupted to turn into sloping rises, and to plunge desperately at the last minute into a devouring sea.

'Nita, look, up here!'

I pulled my thoughts back to myself, listening to the change in the cry of my name. Not a seagull. Something?

'Nita, hey! Here!'

From the house. Up at the window high in the wall I caught movement.

'Oh, Tony.'

I stood up and brushed the back seat of my coat. I moved towards the house, reluctantly. There was nothing good about that house and plenty of reason to stay clear of it. The breakfast bread and margarine I had eaten was all that I wanted of it just now.

'Nita!' So loudly out the upstairs window.

'What's the matter?' I called crossly, 'What?!'

'Look, Nita, look.' He was crying now and beginning to scare me. He was pointing over my head in the direction of the road approaching the house.

Nothing. The seagull was out of sight now.

'Mummy, Nita. Mummy. It's Mummy coming!'

I ran, fell, cried, called, ran and ran and ran.

'Mummy!' I torpedoed into her, my wet eyes, nose and mouth lost in the folds of her gabardine raincoat somewhere around the top of her thighs. My arms locked around her legs. We both nearly toppled over.

'Aah!' she cried, crouching and holding me tight, making funny noises. Somehow a hanky appeared and was applied in a stabbing but methodical fashion to my face, with a couple of surreptitious swipes to hers.

We gathered ourselves up, became orderly and almost digni-fied and headed for the house, with a suggestion in our deport-ment that control had never been lost. I, proudly marching with the visiting mother that was the only one of its species in the area, she, putting on a good face as the more-or-less casual visitor who just happened to be passing by first thing in the morning.

We marched into the house yard; I could see children at the top windows, the early morning sun forcing its way through clouds and highlighting their faces against the blackness of the rooms beyond. Tony was no longer in sight. I turned and looked up at my mother. The sun shone from behind her; her hair glis-tening burnished black and lifting in the wind; her raincoat had become a copper gown in the morning glow. She looked like an angel, radiant, powerful and warm.

. . .

'You get their things together, all of them! You give them to me now or send them to me in London.

'Don't argue with me! I want their vests, socks, pants, everything!'

The angel was transformed, vengeful and violent.

'How should I know where their stuff is now? You know what kids are like. They never know where they've put their things.' Auntie Jean was trying to assemble herself, in dressing gown and in spirit. She made passes at tidying her hair and closing the neck of her nightie. It was a bit early in the morning for her to confront the Medusa.

The other woman of the house had to all intents and purposes turned to stone.

'I want every toy, every bit of clothing, every single scrap that came here with them. If I don't get it all within the week the council will hear from me; I'll report you like a shot. In fact I'd better go now and be done with it.'

She was half Auntie Jean's width at the very most but she had the carriage of a bantam rooster and shared its point of view. Her diction was perfect. I think they understood her.

'Jean, get here!' yelled Auntie Jean up the staircase outside the kitchen door. 'Jeanie!' Jean did not appear, surprising no-one. John wandered in in case something interesting was on.

Something was.

'Go round the rooms and see if you can find any of the toys Nita brought here. Her Ma says she wants 'em. Get going!'

John could see a drama being enacted right here in this room, and like many a dullard, enjoyed watching other peoples' upsets. He went just the same, for fear of life catching up with him in the only intense way it ever did.

My mother was steaming, angry, mortified. My brother Tony had come downstairs and met us at the front door of the house as we had approached it. He stood there in the morning sunlight smiling forlornly, his legs wrapped in filthy bandages, weeping sores showing where the rags had fallen loose. He, like

I, looked like a scarecrow, our hair not having seen a brush in three weeks. Misery had made his body pack up on him again, this time expressing itself through what my mother called 'sand sores'. Each time his skin was broken, it festered. He looked frightful. Many weeks of poor nutrition had exacerbated his problems.

The combination of matted hair, unruly, shabby clothing transferred with the accompanying lice from other children and the mess of would-be bandages, made a picture which, if photographed, would look like something from which Chaplin made sentimental movies. Tony was all too real.

Our mother had taken one look at him and metamorphosed from visiting blithe spirit to vast avenging force, propelling herself and us straight in through the front door and material-ising before a stunned and only half breakfasted Auntie Jean.

Tony and I stayed close, letting her know in an animal way that we were 'with her'.

Putting our bodies against hers, moving when she moved.

'You get all their things together. I want the suitcases I brought, the clothes, the lot.

'I'm going out to get the train tickets for home right now. I'll be back straight away. There'll be Hell to pay if you don't find their stuff.'

She picked up her handbag and grabbed my wrist. 'I'm coming straight back.

'Tony, you'd better wait here.'

She pulled me to the front door and through it. Tony ran after us choking and gasping.

'I want to come too! Please Mummy, I want to come!'

We were outside and moving through the yard.

She stopped, went back to Tony. 'It's your legs Tony, you can't come to the station this time. Mummy is going to come back and get you with the tickets. You wait here; we'll be quick.'

Tony came apart. He stood outside that door with tears streaming down his face, his throat creating great cries of

anguish, his hands outstretched. I looked back at him standing
rooted to the spot. I knew he believed at that moment that he
would never see us again.

A desolate house; a bitter pale sunlight through clouds; a
child alone in a landscape.

That evening in Feltham, when the air raid siren tore at our
stomachs again and the searchlights cut the night sky into triangles and diamonds, spotlighting the fat grey barrage balloons, all
my thoughts were filled with the word, 'Home, home, home.'

I heard our mother murmur, 'If we're going to die, we'll die
together.'

But for Tony and me: we were home, we had our mother,
our house, our safety.

The Hearth

Mummy, Tony and I were by the gas fire in the kitchen.
Mummy was looking grim.

> *'Keep the home fires burning, while your hearts are
>   yearning ....'*

the wireless reminded us.

> *'Though your boys are far away, they dream .. of ..
> home....'*

Winifred was de-lousing us. She had me gripped by the
shoulder with one hand and a fine-tooth-comb in the other. This
instrument of refined torture had been procured the minute my
mother could get to a shop. Deceptively attractive, with its glis-
tening steel neat square shape, decorated on two sides with beau-

tifully precise rows of straight, perfect teeth, it gleamed its threat at me as it descended time and again to grind across my scalp. Exact order was its method, mercilessly scraping in parallel tracks again and again down my skull.

'Ow! Ouch! Ow! Mummy stop!' I yelled blue murder. She was unmoved.

'Keep still! The sooner you let me do it the sooner I'll be finished.' She often said that sort of thing; somehow in my brain it didn't add up to my advantage. She dipped the comb with each sweep into a bowl of foul smelling carbolic and water, drowning her insect victims with expressions of triumph and revulsion alternating across her face. She moved into position behind me where I couldn't see her. The towel around my neck was getting soggy; I smelt of carbolic. I tried not to breathe.

> 'There's a silver lining, through the dark clouds
>   shining,
> Turn the dark clouds inside-out, till the boys come
>   home ....'

It was rather late in the morning for me to be still in my nightdress, but all the clothes from my back the night before were soaking in disinfectant. This is what it means to be lousy apparently. It had something to do with the children in Cornwall. I had in the past been told to keep away from 'those children up the street' because they were 'Dirty,' she said to us, 'Lousy,' she said to her sister, Anne. So the children in Cornwall had something in common with the neighbours up the street. These were in Devon now, lousy or no.

I never got to study a louse, they didn't stay around long enough, so I knew the adjective but never met the owner of the noun. I did see the tiny twiggy corpses floating on the murky white of the carbolic, but couldn't work out what they had looked like when alive, soldiering around in the jungle of my hair. I would have found a louse very interesting to study.

I was fond of insects. Many hours could be passed in peaceful contemplation of their little bodies and legs, their funny, erratic movements. You could actually see their little eyes and their waving feelers when they were working out their next moves. They went forth boldly on courageous adventures, fought against great obstacles, dodged horrific monsters (one of them me I thought, but they didn't seem to know I was even there, I was so big). Sometimes I helped them a bit.

Worms, I have been told, I had the practice of eating when I was very young but mother had taken a dim view of that.

Snails were a delight, since they could be induced to race each other with a little lifting and shifting. In themselves they were beautiful, their soft wet silver-bronze bodies gleaming, the tiny pattern of pearly bumps on their skin dressing them in jewels; they changed their shapes repeatedly, sensing, pausing, reforming; fattening, extending, moving forward. The eye stalks and horns were tiny and perfect, shrinking, waving and growing out and up. How wonderful the shell, with fat spiral roundness decreasing ever smaller to a centre, with radiating lines and ridges around each phase of the spiral in browns, greys and blacks. Under their tummies I could see that it was smoother, paler and sucked upward a bit. And everywhere they went they left their fragile silver trail, each one wandering, looping round, straightening out, then disappearing under a leaf or a piece of wood – if I didn't catch the renegade in time.

The plans I made for them concerned them not at all. I would pick up a specially selected individual, only to have it retreat full speed into its home, or if I was quick, hang about in a daze until I placed it on the running track – invariably a bit of wood spanning the gap between two stones.

What the snail did next had nothing whatever to do with my expectations. I could see that I must police them very stringently if I were to enjoy anything like a race. My contestants left in every direction available to them, and since upside down under the plank was no barrier to their progress, my race usually proceeded in slow, singularly disorderly fashion. I never did get to declare a winner. Since the little creatures didn't know or care that I existed, no-one was the worse for the experience. I had enjoyed their company; they continued on their journeys unafraid.

I could look at a snail for ages. But I never saw a louse. Not alive.

My mother finally finished with me and sat me down with a book by the gas fire to dry. She had polished me off with a rinse of tar soap. This I loved like a drug. I sat on the hooked rag rug as near to the heater as I could, inhaling the intoxicating fumes of the tar soap and idly looking over the pictures of Cinderella after the Fairy Godmother had done her job. I lost myself in dreams of warmth, safety, magic and beauty.

'Tony,' called Winifred, 'You're next.'

I had been waiting outside the house for two hours, looking each way, shifting from one foot to another. Daddy was coming home on leave!

Mummy told me to stay right outside of the house, not to go down the street at all. Daddy will come along just the same.

'That looks like him!'

I broke Mummy's rule and ran, but, no, it was another sailor. They all looked the same at a distance.

I returned to my post outside our house.

'This time it's Daddy!'

I waited till he was right there. He swept me up in his arms and piggy-backed me inside. It was the best weekend ever!

Daddy's hair was very short but he looked exactly the way I remembered him, so I knew him straight away..

Daddy's ship had been somewhere hot with a 'convoy'. They

were sailing with big ships that were going to warm countries for food and supplies. Strange names like 'Egypt', 'Africa' and 'Australia' would come whispering to my ears, although really no-one was supposed to say where they had been, or would go next.

I wanted him to stay. I think he wanted that too, but it couldn't be like that.

On Monday he went back to his ship.

I made a drawing of him, but it wasn't the same as having him here. Mummy looked a bit funny when I showed her.

———

Auntie Anne loomed large in our lives for the duration of the war. She was our mother's older sister, separated by a gap of ten years with five siblings between, two of whom, Tom and Bessie, had died of Tuberculosis during the depression between the world wars.

My Grandmother, Winifred's mother, had died in 1931 when Win was nineteen, taken by a stroke while sitting on the outside toilet.

Auntie Anne had taken the role of parent from that time; she became a key figure in our future mother's life.

Anne was usually crabby.

Life had been hard on her; the protection little Winnie had enjoyed from her older siblings had been unavailable to Anne, now the bossy head of the house. Granddad wasn't there much and wouldn't have cooked and cleaned anyway.

Anne and Win were not alike; not in looks, not in personality. As young women they were both skin and bone, but Anne was all angles while Win was petite and pretty.

Uncle Harry, the older brother, spoilt Win rotten according to Anne. He slipped her pocket money and aided and abetted her escapes through the window to meet her friend Queenie and run off to the Hammersmith Palais to dance with the sailor boys.

It needs to be noted here that it was no disgrace to be seen with a sailor in England.

In 1950s Australia, when I was engaged to my country boy, his navy uniform, newly acquired, marked me as something of a 'tart'.

Not so in England, surrounded by sea and famous for its maritime heroics.

Perhaps Win was a bit of a trial for her older sister.

It was rare for Winifred to snap at us or to be mean to anyone, but when it occurred I heard Anne's voice through her. Auntie Anne used rude words that Tony and I mustn't use. 'Bum', was one. She accused our mother of having, 'Eyes in the back of your bum!' one day when Win sensed what Tony and I were up to behind her. Bert Page, Anne's husband, was a soldier somewhere in Europe.

Anne was a frequent visitor to our home and a constant companion on shopping trips. She never dressed smartly like Mummy always did within the modest budget available, but today her clothing seemed downright careless. Even her hair looked untidy.

'Put the kettle on Win'. Auntie Anne looked crabby again.

'Now, Win, quick for God's sake!'

Mummy looked hard at her sister. Touchy?

I was at the kitchen table building a tower with wooden blocks, just plain ones, not like the 'Victorian' bricks my cousin Joan had when we visited. Hers were coloured, with pieces made to look like parts of the house, a Victorian house, with red painted triangular shapes over the front door and windows, brick painted walls and doors with panels.

Uncle Harry and Auntie Doris were rich. Our cousins, Joan and Dennis, had some very special things that 'cost money'. It wasn't that we were poor, rather that they were rich. Everyone said that Uncle Harry was very smart, and had risen from being a Telegraph Boy to becoming something clever in radio and communications in the army. He was an officer somewhere in the Far East.

My blocks were rising higher. So was Auntie Anne's voice.

'Win! I just don't know what I'll do!'

'For goodness sake Anne, sit down and tell me. It can't be that bad. Come on, I've got a bit of fruit cake left'.

That got my attention. A rare delight. Not for me apparently.

'Win. Oh God, Win. Six weeks since Bert came home on leave. Six weeks'.

She paused. I looked up again.

'I'm pregnant, Win'.

'Pregnant'. A new word. Not a good one. It sounded like Uncle Bert might have done something.

Mummy was stricken silent. She flashed a look at me and back to her sister. She rounded the table and tried to put an arm around Auntie Anne. Anne shrugged her off roughly.

'Bombing, Win. Connie to look after when you're at the office.'

'I'm already getting fat'.

That was true, now that I looked at her.

'It's all very well for Bert; he's gone back to the war'.

This was worse than war? 'Pregnant' was pretty bad.

'Nita, go outside for a bit'.

I looked at my really good tower, but had to leave it.

'Pregnant' changed everything.

Auntie Anne seemed to cheer up a lot when she had a very new baby that she called Patricia. 'Tricia' is what she was always called from the beginning. I loved having her around.

Everyone said what a good, easy baby she was. Perhaps Connie saw it a bit differently; she had had everything her own way until now.

3

GLASGOW 1940

The docks at Glasgow were intensely active. Daddy's ship was in and out of Glasgow from time to time. The Clyde River was an important shipping channel.

Goorock was right next to the docks, where a line of identical tenements offered accommodation at a good price for sailors' wives and families on visits.

We had arrived late at Mrs. Mack's place, Mummy and Tony and I, after a long train ride all the length of England. Mummy was very pleased about this trip – it would give us a break from the bombing. The Germans never came as far as Scotland. There was a limit to the quantity of fuel the bombers could carry in order to get home after they had delivered their load.

'The Blitz' was what they were calling the bombing on the wireless.

This was 1940; I was three and a half and not very interested in the news. I had a brand new packet of plasticine and I had been busy on the train making a family of cats.

Mrs. MacIntosh, more often known as Mrs. Mack, had a houseful of people staying in her solid stone house, with basement, two main floors and an attic, near the waterfront in Goorok. She had an arrangement with the Navy vicar that enabled him to direct visitors to economical accommodation with satisfactory service and filling, if not lavish, meals. This meant that she could keep her little house full and herself comfortable. She liked people around her.

Mrs. Mack reminded me of Mrs.Cooper till she opened her mouth. I couldn't understand a word she was saying. My mother insisted that she was saying real words, just that she was Scottish, that's all.

She was a bustling, busy, cheerful soul, showing us to the very top room in the attic; if we looked out the little window she indicated, we could see the docks fairly close by. She called it a 'wee' window, which amused Tony and me immensely until our mother got cross with us.

Later when she couldn't hear us we whispered jokes about the 'wee' pot under the bed. My mother had the eccentricity to cart one of our heavy china pots with us if ever we traveled. 'You never can tell,' were the words she used to justify this. She herself had fun about the pot. She always called it a 'gazunder' because of its place under the bed. The other name it had was 'The Po'. It was a grand piece of work in its way, heavy cream coloured ceramic with painted roses on it – another subject for irony on occasions. We thought our wee humour both witty and naughty.

Mrs. Mack differed from Mrs. Cooper in another way: she never addressed me directly when my mother was present. She referred to me as if I were invisible. She meant no harm; I don't think she knew she was doing it. Probably it was only her clothes that reminded me of Mrs. Cooper. Or her age. Maybe her body was similar. Perhaps I was just missing Mrs. Cooper.

As soon as I thought of that my eyes watered.

Mummy got along famously with Mrs. Mack. For something to do, she would sit in the kitchen and help with the potatoes. She would go mad without something to do.

My father was to come to Goorok to stay with us at Mrs.

Mack's. His ship was coming in to the Glasgow docks and he was to have shore leave. My mother had been anxious to see him and reassure herself that he was completely well. He was an Able Seaman for the whole of his war service and was a gunner up on the decks. The North Sea was both icy and violent. When he reached my current age, he was deaf as a post.

Location of allied shipping, of necessity, could not be discussed at the time, but Daddy sometimes hinted at his destination. This was close to treasonable.

Winifred had timed the arrival in Scotland pretty well. Walter turned up at the house after only a day had passed.

He frightened me. I didn't know him.

Who was this man with the burgeoning black beard and moustache? With hair growing long over his ears and neck? His face was white and thin; he was buried under masses of navy/black thick clothing but I could see he was skinny.

The sailors needed to grow their hair long as defence against the bitter cold. I had been ashamed to feel my image of his face becoming more and more vague as his absence grew longer, but I knew this was not right, this could not be Daddy.

He clasped my mother. I screamed. He held her tight. What was I to do? I tried desperately to make him let go. Nothing happened. I was helpless against his savage power. My mother! My mother!

Win relaxed, moved back to look at Walter.

'You look terrible, Wal'.

'Well, that's lovely, innit? And I came all this way to visit too! Good to see you love. I'm alright you know.

'I'm here, that's the main thing'.

'We're all here; I don't know how, I'm sure'.

'That's enough of that, Win. We're together for a fortnight and we'll have a nice time. Come on kids, say hallo'.

Tony moved to him, I stayed back. I felt sorry about that, but I had to. I just didn't know him.

· · ·

Breakfast in the house was a crowded and noisy affair with the various guests taking it in turn to ask and answer questions. The morning after my father had arrived he turned up to breakfast transformed: the beard, moustache and long hair were gone. I knew him!

I sat right next to him at the table hanging onto every incomprehensible word spoken by the Scots.

Still the grown-ups talked of nothing but war. There was a difference though: someone would be rattling on about the experiences that they had had, then they would stop unaccountably. I remembered the posters that my mother told me said not to talk, the walls have ears.

LOOSE LIPS SINK SHIPS

So these homesick, weary men and women talked without telling all; shared their time but not their secrets.

They all trotted out photos of their families and were especially good to Tony and me.

One particular lady became friendly with my parents. This led three weeks later to a new episode in my Scottish experience.

Meanwhile, Daddy and Mummy had a lot of catching up to do, so Tony and I roamed the streets - just for a bit of privacy they said. The town was all new to Tony and me so we bundled along looking at everything around the general vicinity of the docks and left them alone.

That evening after dinner Mrs. Mack let me help her with a jigsaw puzzle that was a big picture of Edinburgh Castle, according to the picture on the box. We didn't get much done, just the edge, so you couldn't see the picture in the puzzle yet. We had a quiet evening in Mrs. Mack's parlour.

Amazing! No shelters, no siren, no war! This was Scotland.

I was getting used to Mrs. Mack's way of speaking, with her 'wee' this and 'bonnie' that. I got to like the sound of her voice and the way she rolled her 'R's. There were a number of words she used that I had never heard, but the overall effect of her speaking was a delightful, entertaining and rather soothing one. I was happy to listen to her whether I understood or not. She made no particular fuss of children, but rather was comfortable with them about the house and negotiated around them without apparent effort.

Our attic room was at the top of the house, above the two main storeys, which in turn were above the basement underground.

We climbed up the long staircase to our bed tired but happy.

All four of us were sleeping in the same bed together; that's all we had in the room apart from a massive oak armchair. I went to sleep soothed by the murmur of our parents' voices as they caressed each other with words alone.

Then: 'Can you hear that, Wal?'

'Hear what, love?'

'I can hear a plane'.

'That's O.K. Win, there's sure to be planes around here somewhere'.

'No Wal, that's not one of ours; I mean, I think that's a German bomber'.

'Come on Win, let's get some sleep. You've had a hard time in London, you've got Jerry on the brain. Try not to worry'.

'No Wal. Wal! It's theirs, not ours. A German bomber! I'm sure of it!'

'You're taking this too far, Win, you'll wake the kids. There's no bombing in Scotland, remember?'

Too late. We were well awake; awake and listening hard. The drone was coming closer. There was no doubt. That was 'theirs'. Three of us knew it for certain.

Winifred flew out of bed and out the door.

'I've got to get everyone down to the basement! Get the kids up and out of there.

'Wal! Get out of here! Please!'

Tony was treating it a bit like a scientific test. What was he playing at – The Teacher? He chose now to get a good idea! 'Yes,' he said, 'That's a German bomber.' It was, but I stayed silent, listening to work out where exactly it was in respect to us.

No sooner had my father complained again about the nonsense, than the bomb whistled its way down. A split second after he had thrown himself on top of us, the roof came in.

Daddy moved like lightning to get the fat eiderdown over his back, then kept stock-still, crushing us under his body.

Everything came down on top of us - plaster, timber, slates, brick dust, bricks and wallpaper. We were suffocating from the dust alone. A massive bluestone pitcher had flown through the great hole where the ceiling had been, bounced off the oak chair by the bed and landed across in the fireplace. Our father hazarded a look and interpreted it as an unexploded bomb. He started to remove the covers and extricate us from the mess.

Dust.

Gritty in my nose. My mouth.

My eyes screwed shut; but dust, brick dust, house dust, cement dust.

My father's ear past the dust when I peeped out. How can that be?

My father's hair next to my face, covered with red brick dust.

His shoulder. His heavy weight all over my body. Somewhere my brother whimpering. Somewhere my mother calling our names.

I can't get my arm out.

Now my father moves. The eiderdown lifts and suddenly there's black sky and clouds and stars.

No search lights. No roof either. A great big hole.

Now silence.

Listening.

It was all about listening.

A brick wall separated us from the neighbouring tenement; much the same as any room next door.

The bomb must have entered their roof, lifted everything in its path, to explode upward into the air and land on us. Had the bomb entered our room, we would have been dead. The implication for the neighbours was clear.

Winifred had given up warning the other house guests and had opened our door to come back in, intending to hurry Wal and the kids out of there and down to the basement. At the moment of entering she received a slate to her head, sustaining a nasty wound, thankfully not fatal.

I was not given time to be frightened when the bomb dropped. Terror gripped me in the basement soon after: the vision of the people lined around the wall on benches, their faces white and suspended in the blackness, terrified; shocked by the impossible: a bombing raid on Scotland.

These Scots had had no rehearsal, no warning, no search-lights, no siren, no anti-aircraft guns.

Wal had had no experience of this. He told Win he couldn't wait to get back to his ship.

'It's alright for you, you're used to the bombing. I can't stand it'.

I now believe that Germany must have taken Norway, just 'over the road' from Scotland. Fuel ceased to be a problem for the German bombers for the trip over and back and the Clyde docks were a very important target.

Scotland was no longer safe.

Muthill (Pronounced Mew-thal)

'The skinny pig's had babies! The skinny pig's had babies!'

I tore down the driveway, stumbling, staggering, running like the wind to the cottage where Auntie Mary and Grammer were working in the kitchen.

I had been 'lent' to these ladies after we were bombed out in Goorock. Mummy went back to London with Tony after Daddy returned to his ship. I didn't know why I found myself going to Muthill with the ladies, but things tended to happen like that; it had something to do with the war.

Muthill was not bombed. Yet.

I was often 'borrowed' by people. My future school teacher in the Hammersmith school took me home for weekends. I was easy to manage. Tony, my brother was not, for a variety of reasons which may be coming clear. So Tony went back to London. That was alright.

Muthill, Scotland, and Drummond Lodge fed a ravenous appetite for new and wondrous experiences. While I was contin-uing to be 'manageable', my mind was running riot, grabbing greedily at all stimulation, good and bad, pleasant and unpleasant, safe and risky.

Drummond Lodge was the gate lodge just inside the entrance to the driveway up to Drummond Castle.

The grandeur of that was lost on me; I had been exposed to some vastly different experiences in my few short years.

Drummond Lodge, tucked into an overgrown garden, offered yet another new environment from any I had experienced. It was a small cottage, nothing like the houses in Holly Road and certainly nothing like the bleak white, rectangular evacuation house in Cornwall. Drummond Lodge was a grouping of squarish shapes with steep triangular, tiled roofs here and there, and it had a vegetable garden, flowers and, amazingly, ANIMALS.

My life was transformed by the presence of animals. Not insects, animals!

I had friends.

I could wander the garden and driveway with a black bantam rooster under my arm. He didn't care.

We were always accompanied by a little black Scots Terrier, Jock. The three of us had the run of the place. I had never had a dog or a rooster, though I had visited Mrs. Cooper's cat Sooty as often as I could.

I always left my two friends at home when I went to the castle.

This day I had been visiting the 'castle' children, all older than I was but who allowed me to mix with them sometimes. They lived in Drummond Castle during the time I was staying at Drummond Lodge. They were bigger, with longer legs; I couldn't keep up all the time and can remember following, crying. They took no notice of that, but were kind to me generally.

The fact that I was staying in the grounds of a castle neither surprised nor impressed me; the houses in Goorock and in the

London area were very big and all joined together so I was used to large edifices.

Still, the castles in story books somehow didn't connect to this reality. They had turrets on tall thin towers with pointy tops that reached up into the clouds; they were misty, mysterious and magical. They had princesses in the towers. Drummond Castle was a heavy, strong, solid building, firmly rooted to the ground. And no princess. But it had something the fairy story castles didn't have; it had a Guinea Pig.

The skinny pig had been getting very fat lately, a phenomenon not explained to little girls except in terms of her eating habits. She was eating a lot.

Today the castle children had news for me. I was taken into the castle, up a very large, wide staircase, along a corridor to the right and into a sunny bedroom. A massive wardrobe loomed before us.

Annie, the eldest girl in the group of five, led me forward and instructed me to look into the darkness of the wardrobe. My eyes took a moment to adjust and then I saw them! The skinny pig had little babies – very little! Beautiful little furry babies right next to their mother. All with black and tan and white patches. I was staggered!

I had to report this amazing thing to Auntie Mary and Grammer!

'Grammer! Auntie Mary! The skinny pig's had babies1' Such news to tell; such spectacular new information!

'Hist!', said Grammer, 'Be quiet a moment.'

I held my breath. How could I be quiet?

'Grammer', I whispered.

The wireless was on and Grammer and Auntie Mary were crammed up against it, not cooking as I had expected.

This is the BBC Home Service. Here is the news'. The same as we heard every day in London. Always the same. Stuff about ships, planes, 'actions', peoples' names, allies. Especially the name: 'Winston Churchill' and the strange word 'Nazis'.

My news was different. New news.
I had to wait.

There had been another day when I had news, but not the words
for telling it. At least today I could tell about the skinny pig with
some accuracy.

On the other day I had been out on the driveway with my
two friends Jock and the bantam rooster (who didn't seem to
have his own name.) The sun glinted luxuriantly from his superb
black tail feathers. Iridescent colours fought with each other to
be noticed.

Suddenly, through the open gateway between its two great
stone columns, reeled Grandad on his bicycle.

Grandad didn't live in the gate lodge, He belonged at the
castle with the family. Every day he rode his bicycle into Muthill
to spend his time and money at the pub.

I watched as he wobbled onto the gravel drive, tipped, and
fell onto the grass verge. He thereupon pulled himself up,
mounted his bike and reeled on a bit further.

After a very short trip he tipped again into the ditch under
the whitethorn hedge.

He lay there. It was wet.

He didn't stir.

I went inside and said, 'Grandad's gone to sleep in the
hedge.'

I knew Grandad was dead, but I didn't know the word
'dead'. My mother used many euphemisms. I didn't learn the
real meaning of the word 'pregnant' until I was fourteen.

Grammer and Auntie Mary attended to the Grandad situation, secure in the knowledge that the little girl in their care had
no idea about something she had worked out when she was
barely three.

· · ·

Dinner was a new and strange experience in the cottage.

This day I had a bowl placed in front of me, its contents unrecognisable.

I saw soft white tubes, lots of them, all covered with a white creamy stuff. The smell was enticing, strange but delightful. No potatoes or carrots. No cabbage. No meat.

I had a spoon. I tried a piece, one of the tubes. Delicious! The creamy sauce was made with cheese, local cheese I now think, since, while the odour is still stored in my brain, I know I have never met it again. If we had cheese in London, I can't remember it. The cheese sauce was inside the soft tubes as well as all over it. Very, very tasty!

Macaroni Cheese: to me exotic and unforgotten.

My mother never cooked pasta or steamed rice. There were other food items she would not touch, some of which she served us, but never Macaroni Cheese.

Scotland offered another new delicacy: fresh farm eggs for breakfast, lightly boiled, placed in an eggcup and served with 'soldiers' - toasted bread cut into strips, to be dipped into the egg yolk instead of a spoon. There were spoons if you wanted them, 'Apostle Spoons', very small silver spoons with little men at the end of each handle. I preferred the soldiers.

I had not seen real eggs for a while in London. Powdered eggs were saved with other rations for the occasional fruit cake. Very occasional.

Grammer was trying to move me along one morning as I slowly made my way through the porridge we were having for break-fast. Scottish porridge was a chunky business with more than the tiny pinch of salt that Mummy would put in. I still like porridge the salty Scottish way.

This day we were to go over the road into the woods.

Opposite the gateway to Drummond Castle was an identical set of gateposts: tall stone pillars holding great iron gates. These gates were black and formal, with vertical rods spaced evenly apart to make a secure screen when locked. They were probably pulled down at some stage to contribute iron for the 'war effort', as I know now from a photograph that ornate silver painted gates with scrolled tops feature impressively at the castle's entry and the gate over the road to the woods.

Jock the Scottie dog came with me, following Grammer and Auntie Mary. The bantam rooster stayed back.

We watched as the two ladies rummaged around in the leaves under the woodland trees. Memory serves me with pictures of beeches in Autumn colours.

Grammer had a rake. Surely they couldn't be tidying up the dead leaves? There were just too many, it was a great wide wood. Perhaps they were searching for mushrooms? I knew Grandad wasn't under there; he was taken somewhere closer to town.

They were ignoring Jock and me. We stood at a distance.

I was having a 'lonely day'. It happened sometimes. I stood quietly weeping until Grammer got fed up with me and told me to take Jock home.

As I headed back I fell and cut myself on something. I still feature the scar on my right knee, but Grammer ignored my increased crying. I kept walking back towards the gates, blood notwithstanding. A big toad stared. He was laughing at me. He made me feel even sadder.

Jock and I stood inside the closed Lodge gates, myself holding the black bars and crying.

This was not the image the Scottish ladies held of the little English angel with the blonde curls and a half smile.

They were getting a bit sick of me.

Auntie Mary took me on a walk to the shops on a day soon after this. I held her hand as we walked towards some buildings. A basement and window ahead struck a memory of home.

I said, 'When will I see Mummy?'

Very soon I found myself back in Feltham.

4

FELTHAM 1941

Pearl Harbour

I was settling Blue Teddy into his new bed in a shoe box. Nobody had got new shoes. Mummy had saved the box because 'you never know.'

Teddy only just fitted in it.

Auntie Anne and Mummy were listening very hard to the wireless, looking cross and unhappy. The wireless had just said, as usual, *'This is the BBC Home Service. Here is the news'.*

Never good of course but sometimes worse.

Japan had attacked Pearl Harbour with aeroplanes and submarines. I knew what they were of course, but had no idea about 'Japan' or 'Pearl Harbour' which sounded lovely.

Mummy said, 'Be quiet, Nita', looking upset. She and Auntie Anne made another pot of tea. They had to talk.

Connie and Tony came in and started noticing the atmosphere.

They were quick to display their superior knowledge.

'Japan' is a country, like England,' but it's miles and miles away. 'Pearl Harbour' is, well, somewhere else. It belongs to

America. Connie found a globe of the world. I was four and not yet at the Hammersmith school. This was all new to me.

'The Yanks won't stand for this, Win!' Anne was sure.

'It can bring them into the war, though.'

Until now, the USA had held off declaring war. They had contributed support with supplies across the Atlantic and defence against U Boats in support of merchant ships.

Now America had no choice. The war in the Pacific had begun.

Queenie

Queenie was my mother's best friend. They had gone to school together and gone everywhere else together ever since. There were photos of them in the family album – gay girls striding down the street, taking London and Life by storm, both of them skinny as rakes. There were beach scenes with Winifred in the awful swimsuit she had knitted herself, Queenie in a shiny black article that quite revealed the modest charms she possessed. They featured short bobbed hair, somehow always blowing in a breeze. Their arms seemed permanently linked together, their faces beaming a challenge to the camera and their feet planted firmly so that either one could loll against the other without warning. What a united front they must have presented to the newly discovered combatants – the gay lads that suddenly swarmed around.

The girls were both pretty and sweet with virginal brightness, and a raging success in the dance halls when their Dads would let them go.

Even after Winifred had married her sailor boy, Queenie and she were always in touch. Queenie had no children yet, was not married even, but was not daunted by any need my mother showed to talk about children, prams, rattles and cots, nappy-rash, bottles and colic – these worked on her like the 'shorts' for next weeks Saturday matinee – they made her ache to get on to the real show. There are pictures of her posing with my pram (I presume I was in it somewhere) and standing next to the pond in Feltham holding Tony's hand. They said she was promised to David, who was a soldier somewhere in France.

I sat on the rug near the gas fire in the front room making careful lines on a fresh sheet of paper.

I made a very accurate 'U' shape. I took my pencil in close spirals up the right-hand side, over the top and down the other side. This was hair. I had made the beginning of a face. I began working on the eyes.

'We need some more newspaper, Win,' said Queenie, wrapping the last page around a glass.

The table was buried in wrapped crockery; a box sat in the middle waiting to be filled.

'Where are we going to get that then?' Winifred looked around the room as if paper might appear somehow. Wartime shortages were filtering down to affect the smaller details of everyday living. Newspaper was being used to replace toilet paper. It was lining drawers. It had always gone under the lino on the floors. The Fish and Chip shop and the Butcher had no choice but to wrap their goods in newspapers now, and households commonly tied up their neatly saved, clean stacks and trotted them off to the shops.

'Unless we can wrap the breakables in tea towels or pillow cases? We can do that just before the move.' Winifred was a remarkable manager. Things got done around her, interludes of idleness didn't last long, and diminished resources meant greater resourcefulness.

The challenges of life were grist to her mill. Queenie on the other hand seemed to provide a foil for her. She could point out deficiencies and problems but not make the next step of finding solutions. The two of them were made for each other.

I listened from the floor. I was continuing my set piece of a drawing of a 'lady'. She had a body now, made out of a neatly rectangular chest and an almost triangular skirt. Each line was placed with great deliberation. This was not random creation but exact science.

I knew I had to be accurate. It had to end up looking exactly like a lady.

I had been aware for some time now that my brother Tony did not share my attitude to pencils and paper; they couldn't hold his interest for long. He seemed to prefer finding another boy to play with and retreating to a secluded part of the back yard (or the bedroom on a cold day) and inventing revolting things to do. I never quite knew what they were up to and I used to notice Winifred wearing a quizzical, suspicious expression when she went to find them. I just knew that strangely damaged snails and insects would be left behind after their temporary withdrawals, and that certain of my toys might be altered beyond recognition.

Boys seemed to be that way a bit. I left them alone. In fairness I must say I didn't know any other boys than these. Most were still evacuated. Tony didn't have many boys to choose from. He himself remained a strange animal to me.

My contact with girls was strictly limited. My cousin Connie was always there, frequently with my brother, usually unpleasant for me to be around. I now wonder how her behaviour was influenced by the same war that was driving me into my own mind a lot. She seemed always to be fighting, embattled, or joining Tony in some activity calculated to disturb the peace. With a mother like hers I don't think I would have dared.

On one occasion the two of them were explaining to our mother, 'Nita did it. Look, her name is under it.'

A very bad drawing of a face had appeared on the bathroom wall. Mummy was not impressed and didn't believe a word of it. Apart from the consideration of punishment, I would never have laid claim to such a bad drawing by putting my name under it.

The packing continued with the little paper available.

I was starting my pencil down the length of the lady's arm when the knocker on the front door set up a banging.

'You go Queenie,' my mother said, 'I can't let go of this for a moment.' She was making a knot in a length of string around a box. I got up and ran after Auntie Queenie. My brother appeared from upstairs.

'Who is it Queenie?'

Silence. Queenie had taken some mail from the man at the door and was returning thoughtfully to the front room.

'It was the Telegraph boy. From the Office. With a Telegram. It's a Telegram Win.'

Queenie held it close to her chest as she entered the room. 'Sit down Win. Here.'

Winifred sat.

'You open it Queenie, I can't do it. No, no, give it to me. Give it to me Queenie!' Her face was as white as paper. Her voice was rising to almost a shriek.

I stood between them by the table; Tony stood in the doorway, his friend behind him now.

'Oh, God, Queenie.' My mother voice had dropped to a moan; she took the envelope and opened it. Then in a whisper: 'He's not dead. He's not dead Queenie; he's sick but he's not dead!'

I saw my mother cry for the first time ever. It was a truly terrible thing.

Auntie Queenie stayed in Danesbury Road with Tony and me. We really didn't have a lot to worry us. Daddy was in hospital in Liverpool and Mummy was going to see him. That didn't mean much to me. No doubt it could have conjured up some uncomfortable images for Tony, a veteran of hospital residency, but there was no evidence in his daily activity that he was reflecting on anything, anything at all.

There had been some very bad moments during the hours after the telegram, but my mother's drive to action had soon taken over. Emotional lapses were not allowed. When things go wrong, you pull yourself together.

This is war. Get on with it.

Organisation was stepped up markedly within a short space of time – Tony and I had to get out of the way fast and often. No-one could rise to a challenge like Winifred. Positively every inconvenient, time-consuming emotion was squashed flat. She was cheerful, optimistic. She stopped eating altogether; she simply couldn't get anything down.

For the duration of the war and for some time afterwards, Winifred weighed six stone seven pounds.

We saw her off to Liverpool the very next day.

I went as usual to Mrs. Cooper's house that afternoon and all the other days that my mother was gone, but the visits were different now. I arrived a little bit late that day and Sooty was really very annoying. She ran into my legs so that I fell over on the path. Mrs. Cooper had to put some iodine on my knee, which was terrible. We didn't say much when we had our bread and butter and sugar, just looked. A lump of bread sat unwanted in my hand.

Sooty kept staring at me and made me cry.

Mrs. Cooper got an idea; she had a book she wanted to show me, a small green cloth covered book with a picture on the front of two animals lazing under a huge tree by a river-bank. You could see that they had been picnicking, and had just polished off a couple of serves of pie.

'The Wind In The Willows' by Kenneth Grahame, she said.

It was a book for children, but nothing like mine at home.

The sounds of the words – and the words themselves – were much more marvellous, much better at making you FEEL what was happening. Mrs. Cooper read Chapter One to me that day; and each time I visited she read another chapter, always commencing by saying, ' The Wind In The Willows, by Kenneth Grahame, Chapter what-ever-it-was.'

This was a very enjoyable situation, hearing a story in sections day after day. I looked forward with great pleasure to hearing the next chapter, knowing that I would meet the same little friends again and see what happened to them next. My insect adventures I played in my garden were not as elaborate as those that Mole and Ratty enjoyed.

Mrs. Cooper introduced me to a very different style of story-book and story telling.

Mrs. Cooper filled the days spent away from Mummy with comfort and love in the form of exposure to a writer of distinction. The fact that she timed it right for our house move was a masterpiece of consideration and generosity.

Meanwhile, Auntie Queenie knew exactly what to do around our house; she had it all pretty much packed and labeled by the time our mother got back.

Having Queenie at our place had been a bit of a lark because she didn't know all the house rules. Instead of getting *one* boiled sweet doled out after breakfast each day, we found we could have another only for asking nicely. She was being extra kind to us and spoke in a thoughtful way about our father, who was still very ill with something the North Sea did to him. His ship had brought him back to port – all the way around the top of Scotland just to get him to hospital in Liverpool.

Auntie Queenie wasn't strict about bedtime either, and was always willing to read at least one extra story. You could look at every picture as long as you liked.

Staying awake later meant listening to adult conversation in

Mrs Cooper's shelter, but that was only ever on one subject now. Long considerations about where the Allies were and where the Germans had got to were interrupted by muted remarks about the noises that provided a constant background hubbub.

Such comments as 'That was close,' and 'Wait,' and 'That's alright,' were dropped like full stops and commas throughout an otherwise continuous discourse. Tony and I would have a trumped up fight over a hot water bottle, or a genuine one over our feet meeting together in the middle as we lay one each end of a camp bed.

We were a bit naughty really. I felt as if we were tricking Auntie Queenie; after all, if Mummy had been there, one look would have settled us.

Our mother was a skilled exponent of the 'one look'. It worked equally well at home or out. I can't imagine why, because she never did anything dreadful to follow it up, but what with her tone of voice and her 'look' she had us under perfect control. In my case, both in and out of her sight. In Tony's case, it depended on who he was with when he wasn't where she could see him.

Auntie Queenie didn't have a 'look'. We knew we were getting away with murder and didn't mind at all, exploiting our mother's absence and Queenie's extra carefulness of our feelings. She needn't have worried too much about that; we had no doubt at all that Daddy would get better.

Everyone always did, except of course Grandad, Mummy's father, but he was old so that was to be expected.

'He'd had a good innings,' they said.

'Not a small portion of it spent on the drink,' they also said.

Our father must have been fine. Mummy was writing letters to us, all about the hospital and the place where she was staying with a Mrs. Forbes. She wrote that Daddy had been in the cold too much, that's how he got sick. I could only see him in my mind in a favourite photograph, standing up, looking very healthy and strong. How could I be worried when he looked so well? I sent him my best drawing of a lady.

My father's ship had left Liverpool dockyard pretty much straight after it had delivered him. He spent the next days and nights wrestling with pneumonia. He was very near death. He said that the nurses kept telling him to go to sleep. He said he knew that if he did, he would die.

While he lay in hospital fighting for his life, his ship went down with all hands. Were it not for the pneumonia, he would have drowned along with all his mates.

My mother told us all this when she got back home. As our father improved she had itched to get back to us.

My father was 'convalescing', a new word to add to our vocabulary; yet another special 'war' word.

Winifred and Queenie troubled each other with long talks about coincidence and luck, talks which terrified and fascinated them. At first it seemed too much of a coincidence that saved Wal, that by becoming so desperately ill that he had to leave the ship he had stayed alive! But then they realised that this was not so very different from the coincidences that were happening every day in London. After all, just by deciding to walk home a different way or use a different shelter or not visit your friend in West Ham, you could miss out on a direct hit. Any day of the week.

We had not long ago heard about a house in Penzance. An enemy bomber out of his way had off-loaded his bombs down there and wiped out a whole house and everyone in it. We wondered what house that might have been.

So there we were, sitting in the target zone of bombers, survivors by the grace of coincidence alone.

There must have been a lot of grief and fear about during these times, but I couldn't tell; I was busy with the doings of a child.

Every day brought new wonders. Every day I learned some-

thing new: a new way of drawing, a trick for drawing a battle-
ship or a Scotty dog with only a few straight lines, shown to me
by an uncle on leave. How to colour inside the lines and make
an even all-over shading by doing lots of lines really lightly,
shown to me by my cousin Dennis, who was twelve.

While I was working on my drawing skills, I could ignore
the background noises that played out ceaselessly. Even if Hitler
eased up on London on occasions when he moved his attention
elsewhere, he returned soon enough. While children like myself
were certainly not allowed to watch 'dog fights' in the sky over
the south of England, many other activities murmured in the
background. We became 'deaf' to it.

Ambulance sirens, fire engines, people's voices either on the
wireless or in the street; the clean-up activity of the Air Raid
Wardens, all this was too familiar to attract my attention. Bombs
of course, but even those we could sleep through in our shelter.
Perhaps that was not true for Winifred and Anne. Or Mrs.
Cooper.

The Air Raid Siren always got a response.

Still does in the new century when a stupid and insensitive
advertiser uses it on the television.

My stomach clenches.

Mummy was in Liverpool, visiting Daddy.

This brought back my worries about not remembering him
properly. Since the war started and he went away, I had lost
something of the picture I had in my mind, the picture that was
'Daddy'.

Whenever he had come off his ship for a short leave, he was
nothing like my picture. He was tired and sad. He didn't seem
interested in Tony and me and things were different when he
was with our mother now. He had grown his hair very long
again and wore a full black beard to protect against the North

Sea cold, but even when that was all shaved off he was almost unrecognisable.

I had always thought that he loved the sea and ships. He had told stories about it, making it sound very adventurous, even describing a mermaid he had seen once. I was thrilled by that and reported it to my teacher some time later, when she had told the class that there was no such thing as mermaids.

'Miss Robertson, my daddy has seen a mermaid!'

A heated debate ensued. Normally I would not argue with a fierce authority like Miss Robertson, but my daddy's reputation was at stake.

Learning that 'there is no Santa Claus,' was nothing against my facing up some years later to the fact of the false information my father had fed me. I learned over time that, unlike Winifred, Walter had a vivid imagination and a love of making up stories. While uneducated, having left school at fourteen for the same reasons that had pressed Winifred into earning a wage, Walter was the possessor of a strong creative drive, untrained but eager

This had been curtailed by his war experience on board ship, but by no means stifled.

During his hours not manning the guns on deck or keeping himself and his clothing clean, my father worked with his hands on sewing, knitting and craftwork. He brought home samples of this when we saw him. There was a pretty but odd concoction of embroidery silks made up into dressing table mats with tufted 'flowers' all over them in pink and pale blue.

This sad, tired man brought his offerings home to a family that he too must have felt to be slipping away from him.

'Mrs. Cooper, Mrs. Cooper!'

No answer. I tore out of the front gate, around the side lane and into her back yard. She was filling the coal scuttle from the bin. She looked cold, her finger tips poking redly out of her fingerless gloves, her face nearly lost in the folds of her woollen hat and scarf.

The coal bin loomed black behind her. It was a four sided metal affair with the front partly missing. A large square lid hinged down from the top back at an angle, but this stood open now. For some reason I loved the coal bin. It excited me: great shapes made out of smaller ones; shiny black coal lumps with broken sharp edges; flat planes catching the little light there was and flashing it back to me. Dusty granules in crevices; messy black on your hands. And the smell! And how much dust up your nose?

Mrs. Cooper's cat suddenly materialised half way down the pile. Black as pitch, imaginatively named Sooty, she followed Mrs. Cooper everywhere.

'Come on Sooty, get out of the way! Oh, hello Nita, where did you come from? This silly cat thinks I'm playing with her and I'm freezing to death out here.' She hefted the filled coal scuttle by its hinged handle, her shoulders tilting steeply in the effort. She looked older than my mother.

'Come on inside where it's warm. Come on Sooty, you silly girl.'

I picked Sooty up. She took this indignity in good part, not being old enough a cat to have expectations related to her status. She hung happily on either side of my two hands, boneless as an empty sock.

'Mrs. Cooper, I came to tell you, we're moving!'

I stood close by her at the stove as she turned the gas on under the kettle. No doubt I got in her way, but she never murmured.

'We're moving to Hammersmith Mrs. Cooper. Tomorrow!' This was not strictly true, but it was all tomorrow to me if it wasn't today.

'Well, I did hear your Mum saying something like that. But I expect you know more about it than I do, so tell me, where's Hammersmith?'

'Mummy says it's in London.' I had to think quickly to keep the story going; I searched my mind for detail.

'To Mrs. O'Neill's. Mrs. O'Neill's got a cat, Mrs. Cooper.'

'Well that's a good thing for sure, because you might not see so much of Sooty now. I know she'll miss you, she needs someone young to play with.' This point of view was not supported by Sooty who had taken her fickle affections off and was hunting imaginary dragons behind a towel on the clothes horse. The clothes horse fell.

'That's that then, you silly cat,' laughed Mrs. Cooper, tossing her out the door into the passage, 'I expect you'd like a cocoa, then?' She spoke to me over her shoulder as she closed the door.

Her kitchen looked a bit different from ours, a bit messier I suppose, but a bit newer too. She had a gas stove in her scullery, a little longish room off the main kitchen. She still had a big iron stove under the chimney in the main room, but I think she mostly used it for heating. The lino on her floor looked worn near the doorways but she had put a nice big rug in the middle of the room and it covered nearly the whole floor. One thing I liked was the pile of books she always had on the big round table in the middle of the room. I couldn't read of course, although I could follow my story books quite well, what with the pictures and the fact that my mother had read them to me so often.

Mrs. Cooper's books were a sort I hadn't seen before. They looked a bit like each other, some of them. I would look over the edge of the table and try to see the pictures on the front. The front covers always had amazing pictures of strange places and people. 'Detectives', she told me, 'Agatha Christies, Who Dunnits.' I had no idea what she was talking about; I just knew that Mrs. Cooper seemed to me to be very lucky to have so many books and to have the time to read them.

When I'm grown up I'm going to do that. Mummy says she hasn't got time to read in the daytime. When I'm grown up I'm going to do that too!

The pictures on Mrs. Cooper's walls were not really pictures I suppose. There was a calendar near the stove, and a picture frame with a poem in it on the far wall – 'If', which told you all the things to do if you wanted to be a man, which I didn't and from what I understood, I couldn't either. Still, the poem had a nice painted edge around it. Then there was a black cut-out side view of a face. Mrs. Cooper said that that was one of her Relations. Apart from these things there were all sorts of ornaments around the room, lovely things like cats and dogs and horses made of china, and real shaped china flowers on top of a little china bowl. There were plates that weren't used for eating dinner, you just looked at them hanging on the wall.

My mother didn't have all these things around; she called them 'dust collectors.' Whenever I was at Mrs. Cooper's I went all around the room touching her things and she never said a word.

Mrs. Cooper was so special to me. A private place where I could go and talk and not be treated like a child. Of course she knew she was big and I was little, but she was different about it. She was the only one I knew who found what I said important. And she tended to answer the very thing I said, whereas other people seemed to skip straight from what I said to something they were waiting to say; it never made sense. She was the only older person I knew who listened, stopped to think first, and then spoke. And she didn't use a different voice for me either like my Aunties and Uncles, who really looked and sounded a bit strange, trying to make me believe that they had time to look at a drawing or a dolly's dress. This was even more annoying when I hadn't wanted to be interrupted in the first place.

However was I going to manage without Mrs. Cooper. I could pretend that I thought of this at the time, but it never occurred to me at all. There, with my thick china cup of cocoa with the picture of King George and Queen Elizabeth on their wedding day, a lump of 'bread pudding' in my hand and Mrs. Cooper over the table from me, I was the ultimate hedonist, lost in smells and flavours and the sight of my lovely friend, her silver-black hair with its soft Celtic wave, her black smiling eyes and her round rosy cheeks.

I studied her. I wanted to remember her. I looked over her plain brown wool shirt and olive green cardigan, her straight skirt, dark donkey brown, and her cream cotton pinny. She didn't dress like Mummy and Auntie Queenie at all. Her shoes were flat and chunky like mine, with warm navy blue stockings.

Her hands on her cup had suffered from the cold. She still wore her fingerless gloves, so I could see her chilblains. She smiled broadly at me. She looked so lovely.

'Isn't your Daddy due to come home on leave in a month, Dear? I know your Mummy was wanting to get the move over before he came. Well, won't he be pleased to have a break then?'

Daddy. I sort of remembered him. I never dared to say to anyone that I had lost the picture of him in my mind. I could still summon up his size and shape, his sailor's uniform, his kit bag. We had photographs of him and I could visualise those, but in truth I could not see his real face anymore. This was too awful to say.

'My Daddy's coming.….' The sentence didn't have a finish to it. I looked at Mrs. Cooper, hoping for help.

'Ah, well, I wonder what he's going to think of our shelters and things? I wonder where he's been. I'll bet he'll have some stories. My Mr. Cooper went into the army. I got a postcard from him.

'I bet your Daddy's going to have some stories, and won't he get a surprise to see your new house?'

'Yes, yes, and my brother's going to start a new school. I want to go, but Mummy says they won't let me yet and she needs me to help her. I went to the Chiswick school before, to get me out of the way. They've got crayons and plasticene at school, and blackboards and slides and see-saws. I really, really want to go! I'm getting big now, so they could let me. Maybe.'

Mrs. Cooper looked at me for a moment.

'I wonder, Nita, if you could let me have one of your drawings to keep? And I've got a camera. Maybe we could take a picture of you with Sooty? I could put it on my sideboard with Mr. Cooper. Up there. We could ask your Mummy to take a picture of both of us.'

'I expect she would like that Mrs. Cooper.' The situation seemed to call for formality.

'I've got a drawing you can have, or I could make you a special one if you like. Of Sooty. I've got a new black crayon.'

'Thank you Nita. Then I'll have that here after you move, but I still want you to come and see me, you and your Mum. Don't forget, will you?'

Never, never, never could I forget Mrs. Cooper.

My father's visit came and went. He brought us things he had made and talked to Mummy and Auntie Anne a lot. The 'Daddy' that used to play with us had gone. Deadened somewhere in the North Sea.

He had his adult preoccupations on board ship, including the running of a 'Pontoon School', Pontoon being a card game that also supplied opportunities for gambling. He made money on this with his uncanny awareness of the cards that other players must be holding. He would not need to cheat by marking the cards. He was perhaps practicing what the casinos nowadays call 'card counting' and get very nasty about it.

Years later, when we all played cards on Saturday nights, he could defeat us at 500 or poker and his high level of skill at Solo Whist.

Years later, my mother played Solo at her nursing home with great skill.

5

HAMMERSMITH 1941

Our move to 22 Bridge Avenue, Hammersmith went without too much trouble. There were few men around to help, so our mother had to pay a man with an old van. We were moving into the home of a lady whose husband was no longer there. That was not explained to me. We had only two rooms, and a kitchen which we shared with Mrs. O'Neill.

I have few, but very fond memories of Mrs. O'Neill.

She may have liked having me there, because she gave me a very beautiful doll she had dressed. It was always called 'The Victorian Doll' and I never gave her another name. Her dark red dress and white cotton underwear, her stockings and her shoes were perfect. Mrs O'Neill had made every stitch of it. I couldn't see how anyone could do such fine work. Her dress was long and slim, with narrow pleating vertically across the chest and horizontally around the bottom of the skirt. I thought it very smart.

She was an 'old fashioned doll,' my mother said; Queen Victoria's time.

She had long cotton bloomers that opened at the back so that she could use the pot. Mrs. O'Neill said a real lady probably would have had a 'commode,' which was a wooden box with a lid and a pot in it. I wished I had one of those for my doll, but I didn't say so.

The stockings she wore had a pale blue and white Scottish diamond pattern and came right up to her knees. Her knees were strange. So that they could bend, they were cut through nearly to the back. You never really saw them, so that was alright. The parts of the cut were lined with cotton fabric so you didn't see her sawdust stuffing. She had 'china' hands, face and feet.

The most magical thing about her was her eyes! They were made of glass and were REAL. I gazed into them for long minutes at a time. She had neat fair hair and a floppy red hat. I never again held a more wonderful doll.

Months later Mrs. O'Neill let me have some lilac flowers from her front garden to take to school. The intoxicating smell of lilac is always the smell of Mrs. O'Neill.

A Letter from France

'Queenie! Queenie! Read this. This letter from Wal! I can't credit it; how he can write such a thing. To ME.'

Auntie Queenie came by quite often. She was a comforting listening ear for Win, more so than Win's older sister as she understood Win's temperament a lot better. Neither of them remembered I was in the room. I kept still.

'It's all right, Win. It can't be that bad. Come on. It's good he writes when he can.'

'No it bloody well isn't!' I couldn't believe my ears.

'I don't need this!'

Auntie Queenie had the letter now. She read it through. And again, slowly. 'Oh'.

'He wants to know if I know how to get an abortion. An ABORTION, Queenie!

'He's got a French girl pregnant!'

What's that? 'Pregnant?' That word? I'd heard it before.

Something Uncle Bert did on leave. Something bad. Now Daddy's done it.

'Abortion?'

Daddy's asking Mummy to fix it. He's a long way away so what does he think Mummy can do? Mummy's very clever, but I don't think she's going to want to fix this from the sound of her.

Who's this 'French' girl? Daddy knows her. Mummy doesn't.

I don't think Mummy's going to help.

Auntie Queenie and Mummy poured themselves a sherry.

In the middle of the day?

They drank in silence and left me wondering about this thing called 'pregnant.'

Wal was fond of saying, 'Any port in a storm. All storms.'

It was repeated at odd times all his life.

His phrase apparently explained things that needed clarifying, and had not meant a lot to me until I saw an old wartime photograph of him in uniform with another sailor.

They both smiled at the camera, obviously good mates, which came somewhat clearer to me as I grew older and more knowing. Dad was young and very handsome. His friend was leaning over to place his forehead against Wal's with a blissful, dreamy gaze at the camera.

He was, without doubt, in love with my father.

Winifred at ninety-two in her Retirement Village flat studied the old photograph.

She said somewhat vaguely, 'I often wondered about that friend of Wal's.'

Any port in a storm.

Shipboard loneliness and misery could be alleviated.

I was able at last to go to Ravenscourt School. I had had such happy memories of the school in Chiswick, where I could draw pictures and make plasticine fairies.

My first experience of the Hammersmith school was disastrous.

I had dressed quickly, desperate to leave, even willing to walk to school with my brother. I had my lunch with me. Mummy had packed lunches for Tony and me. This turned out to be a catastrophe.

We were assigned a classroom. Even with the Evacuation there were many children attending the London schools. Many mothers had made the same decision as Winifred and brought their children back from their evacuation houses, perhaps for similar reasons, or perhaps to relieve their own loneliness.

Our room was full. We sat, Tony and I, at a small wooden table, opposite each other on little wooden chairs.

So far so good.

After some preliminary welcomes, especially for me, the new girl, some general information about the day's activity followed.

The teacher said, 'We don't need lunch. We finish at lunchtime this week and go home.'

I was horrified. Even terrified. My first day and I was doing something wrong! I held my lunch bag under the seat to hide it. I looked around the room. Could anyone see my illegal lunch? Tony didn't care at all, but that was normal for him. He was quite used to doing the wrong thing, but also more familiar with school rules and consequences.

How could I dispose of the evidence? You positively couldn't throw food out!

Then followed an appalling stretch of time during which I tried to eat the offending lunch, just to hide it.

Crying, stuffing a sandwich in my mouth, keeping my head down to hide my face.

The special classroom photographer was asking me to smile. His job was to record the happy kiddies in their happy class.

'Don't cry Nita, we want a smile don't we?'

'Stop crying Nita! Stop it! Shush. Stop crying!' Tony was mortified to be seen with me.

I didn't know how to ask to go for a wee and I wet my pants. And the chair. And the floor.

Somehow the morning was endured.

Soon the days at school settled into a pattern. I learned what to me were the rules: this you do, this you do not do. As I grew older I was able to see things a little more flexibly, but was ever the cooperative schoolchild, mostly for fear of consequences but sometimes with actual enjoyment.

The pleasure of school was tainted. The war was ever present. Huge concrete pipe sections were put in the playground. We were told they were there for us to get inside if the bombing started while we were outside.

On one occasion the whole school body was moved to a ground level room with rows of seats all facing one way. This was so that we could be entertained during the raid.

In addition, all the children from St. Paul's had to attend our school, because their school was bombed out. We were crowded.

I remember two plump boys singing, *The Quartermaster's Stores* ...

> *'There were rats, rats, big as blooming cats, in the*
> *Quartermaster's Stores'*

... accompanied by the sounds of anti-aircraft guns in the distance.

School, indeed Life, was conducted to an orchestral backing of war.

As the war progressed, concern grew regarding the nourishment of children.

I can now see that the solutions found, not only by my own mother, but by the school - or its parent body – quite possibly fed us up with a diet far superior to the one that I see some children consuming here in the new millennium.

Our food was limited, plain and fairly healthy.

Certainly there was nearly no meat around. My mother queued on a Friday for two hours to get one rabbit. So we had a largely vegetarian diet. I've reached over eighty years of age, in pretty good health (give or take) so something must have been right.

Once a week we were offered a supplement. We queued quietly for our turn.

This week the Smith twins, two horrible boys who did every-thing together, had apparently caught the same cold.

I was trying not to stare at the 'candles' running down from each of their nostrils. 'Candles' was the name given by Mummy to the green muck channeling down to their mouths. I had to stare. It was fascinating. If the twin sniffed, the candles flew out in front, retreated up the nose, then landed back where they started.

When the queue moved on I couldn't watch anymore.

Anyway, I was more interested in the treat we were waiting for.

Coddliloroilamalt. An awkward name to say.

Cod Liver Oil and Malt.

I was clutching my 'ship hape'ny,' a beautiful halfpenny copper coin with a sailing ship on one side and King George on the other. For a hape'ny we were fed a teaspoonful of Malt Extract which I adored. I would have had more and more if they'd let me.

School dinners were a different matter ('dinner' was the name for the midday meal back then and 'tea' for the evening meal, at least in our circles).

We were all seated at very long tables, one each side of the main hall. Plates were brought to us and plonked down with the clear implication that choice did not come into it. Eat what you're given. As usual.

On one occasion we were confronted by that rare commodity: meat, along with the cabbage, carrot and potato. This foreign looking item was part mutton but mostly fat. Even as I look back, I can't name the cut of meat. Not a chop anyway; no bones.

Fat was precious during those years, usually saved, boiled, clarified, separated and used for cooking. This clarifying resulted in a delicious brown residue in the bottom of the pudding basin, a treat that you could spread on bread – after fighting your brother for it. The fat, the bread and the desired residue were known as 'bread and dripping' and provided one of the very few snacks available.

Long, chunky fat attached to meat on your dinner plate was another matter. We schoolchildren were now so unused to it that it made us feel sick just to look at it.

The rabbit our mother had sometimes queued for had no fat on it at all. Sometimes she got liver, but no fat on that either.

I don't know where the dog came from under our table, but he was a godsend, more than willing to dispose of the nasty greasy strips we handed him. Teachers and mothers supervised us closely to make sure everyone was getting the hard-won nutrition, but we managed to smuggle much of it under the table.

Another mysterious substance was fed to us at a subsequent school dinner.

The vegetables on the plate could be recognised, being the ubiquitous potato, carrot and cabbage.

The strange new substance had the appearance of mincemeat in gravy, but smelt disgusting; not like food at all.

Teachers and mothers had their work cut out to get any of it into us. It tasted horrible!

We were accustomed to eating what was given us; in wartime, choices were limited and you took what you could. We were used to being a bit hungry most of the time. We hardly knew the difference.

But this was impossible. How to get it down your throat?

Much later, when my first baby was weeks old, I was expected to put vitamin drops on her tongue.

The first time I did this, apart from the baby recoiling from the shock of the alcohol suspension, I myself recoiled, recognising that smell immediately!

That revolting mincemeat at school dinner had been liberally laced with a multi-vitamin tonic.

The supplement might have done well for us if only we had got it down.

Women were bonding together ever more closely.

One morning we headed off along Bridge Avenue, Mummy, Auntie Anne and I; Anne's daughter Connie and my brother Tony were at school. I don't know why I was home.

Auntie Anne was pushing the pram with Tricia, her baby, in it.

A dreary day weather-wise, but that doesn't tell us the season – although summer was usually constant and fine.

We headed away from the river towards King Street, Hammersmith, on the footpath opposite Mrs. O'Neill's. Not far along we were seeing on our left, the 'Mansions', the line of matching apartments that stretched from Mrs. O'Neill's to an alleyway further up.

On our right were houses like Mrs. O'Neill's: tall, with high ground floor iron balconies and important steps leading up to a big front entry. There was a space under the steps and a narrow cement gap between the basement window and the retaining wall of the small area garden. Next to the gap under the steps was a separate entrance door, not grand, probably for servants and tradesmen in the heyday of the house.

There were the 'first and second floor' living levels above the basement, and attics under the roofs with little balconies of their own. They were something like the tenement in Scotland where we had been bombed out, but rather more grand. Had been quite grand once; now more than a bit weary looking.

Out front of one of these houses, at 29 Bridge Avenue, was a large notice-board with 'TO LET' painted on it. This was attached to the iron front railing fence that would soon be confiscated for the war effort.

The notice attracted the attention of the two sisters.

The decision took no time at all. Both families would move in and share, at least until the end of the war - which no longer looked like 'ending by Christmas' as claimed by the hopefuls a couple of years back.

Our little family had less to move in than our Auntie's, which was just as well, as we were to have the top two floors: the attic and the floor below it, called the 'second' floor.

Auntie Anne, Connie and Tricia moved into the basement and 'first' floor.

We all used the imposing front door.

'Imposing' it was, but blown in twice before the war ended.

I watched daily as my mother laid new lino in the attic kitchen, changed a fuse for the electricity and wallpapered a wall.

I learned early that women could do everything.

Years in the future, when the word 'liberated' was bandied about, I had never needed it myself, though I didn't begrudge it for others.

English women did things. They had always just 'got on with it.' Nor were they the only ones in Europe, Australia and the world.

My mother's generation and through them, mine, set the pattern of change that would stir society and challenge stereo-typed gender roles forever.

If the women didn't fix it, it didn't get done. To do it well pleased them.

The first signs of trouble from this development came when the men returned after each of the world wars. Their women had changed. They had become independent. 'Too bloody independent', I heard a male neighbour say.

Auntie Anne didn't lay any lino or do much other than the usual housework. I don't remember her knitting or machine sewing. She didn't make things.

While we still lived with Mrs. O'Neill, Auntie Anne had produced a baby girl and I liked nothing better than to help with her. They said what a good nurse I would be when I grew up. I felt proud. I knew I was good at that sort of thing. I worked the baby into my hospital games. She just had to lie there; I did the rest, working around the hospital, healing people and such ...

Not long after the move, I fell in love.

My cousin John was eighteen and in Army uniform. The age difference didn't matter to me because I didn't know it was love, nor did I know that age was an issue. John was a soldier and desperately handsome and charming. He was my father's brother's son and featured the family eyebrows, like perfect black feathers lain horizontal over perfect blue smiling eyes. His nose was straight and small like Daddy's and his mouth always talking, laughing and singing. I fell in love for the very first time - if you didn't count my father, and that after all was just daddy love.

'Ding, ding, ding went the trolley,' he sang as he sat me on his knee,

'Clang, clang, clang went the bell,' I could smell his young male skin. I put my hand up around his neck where his closely trimmed hair was soft and tickly. I held on to one of his shiny brass buttons and studied his face closely as he talked with my mother.

'Zing, zing, zing went my heart strings,
'From the moment I saw him I fell.'

Well, I don't suppose it was a coincidence that he looked a lot like my missing father, but to my young neglected heart he was all that was wonderful and handsome and strong. He was good to me too, never becoming impatient with the small thing that hung around, which was not bad going for an eighteen year old male on leave for the first time.

'Nita, leave John alone, dear, he's going to get fed up if you pester him.' I looked at my mother with what I hoped was restraint. Why did she care? John wasn't her friend after all.

John was only in London for a week and I didn't see him again until after the war, by which time he was out of uniform and had other fish to fry. I too had other passions, but John would always be, without him ever knowing it, my first great love affair.

We had a new shelter to go to in the street, a public one with lots of other people. Bunks lined the left-hand wall as you went in and seat benches lined up on the right. Parents took bedding in with them so that families could be bundled in somehow to sleep. My mother would put us to bed at home quite early, 4pm, then dig us out when the siren went, wrap us up in blankets and, rain or no, cart us over the road to the shelter in the blackout.

This pattern of bed/get up/go out would stay with me for many years in the form of sleep-walking. Getting up when asleep became a pattern through my teen years and into adulthood.

Only rarely did I sense that it had happened; more often than not my mother or a friend would tell me next day what I had done.

Another profound effect was a lasting abhorrence as a parent for getting my own children up in the night or wrapping a blanket around them to go out after dark.

Auntie Anne was battling with her baby, Tricia, with Connie and all the necessary baby things. Connie was fed up with the baby by now and making herself as difficult as she dared. Her mother had spoilt her for years, not by giving her things, but by giving in to her. Connie was allowed to answer back and to say anything she liked to her mother. Then again, we used to hear Auntie Anne say some pretty shocking things to Connie. I had never before heard spiteful talk between mother and child, and was astounded by the cruelty of it.

Patricia was the baby now. Connie had been replaced.

Now that she had a new chick, Anne's treatment of Connie deteriorated to the point where the girl couldn't do a thing right. I didn't feel sorry for her; it was about time something happened to sort her out.

Our mother had a special problem each night: which child to carry as she belted over the road to get to the public shelter; I usually got the vote. Tony had to wake up and walk.

My father wrote each week from Liverpool. He was getting stronger and with it, bored and lonely.

6

HAMMERSMITH 1942

The Mansions

'That one was close.'

Mummy and I gazed at the red front door, lying on its back in the hallway. It looked sad, as if it didn't know what it was doing there.

We edged around it to get out of the empty doorway and onto the concrete landing at the top of our steps.

Over the road The Mansions were gone, flattened to bricks and rubble. The whole of that side of the street had been wiped out in one go. The likely target was Hammersmith Bridge; we were very close to it. The bomber pilot must have let his load, his 'stick of four', loose too soon. Boom, boom, boom, boom. He ran out of incendiary bombs before he made it to the bridge.

All that happened to us was the flattening of the front door. Another near miss.

Window glass had, for some time now, been criss-crossed with sticky tape to discourage breakages.

It didn't occur to me to think it could just as easily have been our side of the street that was flattened.

I was wondering about the shrapnel we could hunt there.

That was a particular hobby now, collecting shrapnel in the back garden. We had started when the men were digging the ground up for our Anderson Shelter. Grandad Baker was helping. We were finding scraps of twisted metal and getting in the way.

'There must be some good shrapnel in there, Mummy.'

Our hobby wasn't popular with our mother. She made it clear that on no account could we go to the Mansions bomb site. Shrapnel was sharp. The rubble was dangerous. There were places where you could fall into the basement.

Some weeks later we saw a boy with a great jagged, bleeding hole in his forehead from a fall in the same rubble. He and his friend had been rummaging for shrapnel and other treasures. Both were stunned and crying for help. Tony and I watched from our dining room window. People came.

We often stood and watched from the front window at the passing scene. We were at the first floor window, the one above the ground floor that had steps up to the front door.

On one occasion the baker's horse and cart were parked in front of the Mansions bomb site. The baker may have had a delivery van before the war, but vehicles like that had often been reassigned. He now had a covered-in wooden van like a gypsy caravan, with 'BAKER' painted on both sides.

The horse was placid enough; he probably knew the routine by heart. No surprises.

A rare car came along the road as a variation in the action. This was a bit unusual.

It was either a T Model Ford or something very like it, with a very square main body and a vertical windscreen.

The baker's horse turned his head to see. The car windscreen smashed into his face, knocking him unconscious. He lay in his harness on the road, with blood streaming from his nostrils.

We rushed for Mummy, yelling,

'Mummy, Mummy! The baker's horse is hurt, he's fallen down on the road! He's bleeding. Mummy!'

She grabbed towels and rocketed out the door.

Thank goodness she was home! It must have been too early for the Post Office.

The injury to the horse shocked us more than the collapse of The Mansions.

We had become inured to bomb damage. Even on the scale that faced us over our own street.

Our side of the street was still intact. I was allowed to push my dolly's pram along our side of Bridge Avenue (away from the bridge) towards King Street. There was an awkward detour I could take if I wanted to, via Angel Walk. This narrow alley ran behind the pub, 'The Angel', on the corner of Bridge Avenue and King Street.

I hope that charming pub and alley were preserved. Angel Walk was cobbled, so made interesting passage for myself and the pram. The Angel itself was a very small pub, and very popular. Pubs in England provided companionship and recreation at a time when morale was important.

The Angel was always crowded. Women were, of course, welcome in the bar. I say, 'Of course', because in August 1948, when our migrant ship, the Asturias, stopped in at Freemantle in Western Australia as our first sight of our new land, my mother was shocked to be evicted from the bar she had entered with Dad.

More shock came with the news of Six O'Clock Closing, bringing with it the Six O'Clock Swill, the race to fill up with beer before being thrown out. Civilised drinking was a long way in the future for Australia.

The Anderson Shelter

The siren sounded early. The days were getting shorter.

I was working on my family of cats made from my store of plasticine. This had no separate colours anymore and was a uniform grey/brown throughout.

Life had slipped into its familiar pattern of evening air raid siren and unrushed movement to our Anderson shelter. I was home. I had my plasticine, my drawing paper, my pencils, my Victorian doll and my blue teddy. Most of all, I had my mother.

Our own newly acquired Anderson shelter was a great adventure. At first. It soon became routine. What was initially a novelty suffered the fate of most novelties by becoming commonplace.

Our father had brought home a ship's hammock on one of his rare appearances. We seldom saw him.

When he appeared he was changed; he was no longer the warm, laughing Daddy we had known.

This man was distant and quiet. He was still shocked by our Air Raids.

His ship, The Chitral, had been traveling in convoy to Canada protecting Merchant ships picking up essential supplies. The Atlantic, the Mediterranean and the Indian oceans were studded with enemy U boats, but somehow those dangers were preferable for our father to the certain arrival nightly of bombing raids on Londoners, who lacked a vast ocean in which to hide.

The hammock was cut in half lengthways and strung up on either side of the shelter. Tony and I had one with our feet meeting annoyingly in the middle. Connie and Tricia had the other. The two mothers had a mattress on the floor. If Daddy or Uncle Bert turned up, they had to sit up in the small space left.

The walls and roof of corrugated iron arced over our heads. The door at one end was only just big enough. Our haven was lit by a hurricane lamp before bedtime and a very small spirit lamp overnight.

I would go to sleep with my eyes on the perfect little spirit lamp that gently lit the shelter near my face. My child's eyes found magic in the frosted glass globe, only one and a half inches high on a delicate metal base which held the liquid fuel. I trailed my eyes around the bottom of the glass globe. The castellated metal was golden and delicate. I sank into sleep, vaguely aware of explosions booming through the earth.

In the 1970s, in Melbourne, Australia, I sat in a movie theatre watching the film, 'Where Eagles Dare'. I did not know how very well I had stored the memory of explosion through rock, till the end of the movie when the citadel was blown up. Quadraphonic sound.

I was transported back in time in abject terror. Once in a while a sound or a smell will show me the true effect of the war on a child mind.

One night, Mummy was late getting to the shelter and the bombing had started. She copied one of our games. We used to play 'Air Raid'. We tipped over a massive leather club lounge in Auntie Anne's kitchen and that was our 'shelter.' Mummy told us after the raid that she had done exactly that.

Bread Pudden

The house was empty except for the baby and me.

Tricia was asleep in her cot and I was sitting on one of the brass coal boxes that lived either side of the big iron stove in the main basement kitchen. I was busy tidying up my Victorian doll. Not that she ever got in much of a mess.

Auntie Anne was hanging washing in the brick paved area out the back. That's where the clothes line had to be because the Anderson shelter dominated the grassed area further out, up three brick steps. Some of the remaining space up there was taken by vegetable plots.

My mother was at the Post Office, but it must have been Saturday, because I was not at school and Tony and Connie had gone for a walk to Ravenscourt Park. I never went there without Mummy.

Mummy would be home soon and we'll all have dinner at about twelve thirty.

It occurred to me that I could do something useful. I could slice the bread ready for dinner.

I went into the scullery, where the loaf was sitting on the

bread board. I got the bread knife and carried it all through to the table in the main kitchen where I could manage better.

They'll be surprised to find the bread all ready.

I lifted the knife and placed it across the hard top of the loaf. Now, I knew from watching Auntie Anne, you saw it back and forth to cut through the crust.

That went well so I kept going. I held the loaf tight, sawing through the softer bread.

Trouble! The knife veered off askew as it cut down, ending up with the slice diminishing to nothing. I had no idea this was so hard to do!

I had another go, being very careful how I held the loaf whilst I was sawing.

Disaster! Another messed up slice. I looked at the carnage and did the only possible thing, just as Auntie Anne came back inside I was putting the ruined slices into the food waste bin.

'What do you think you're doing with that bread, Nita?' she shouted.

Red faced, panicked, I cried, 'I was helping, Auntie, and it didn't work.' Tears were starting.

'Get away from that! Do you imagine we can throw bread out? There's a war on. Bread is rationed! Wicked, wicked girl!'

I cringed away. I knew that she smacked Connie. Will she actually smack me?

She rescued the mangled bread and dumped it on the scullery bench. I got out of there and up to our own kitchenette in the attic as fast as I could mount the three flights of stairs.

I was still sitting doing nothing on a chair facing the door when Mummy got home; she came into the kitchen carrying a bowl with the evidence. I was mortified – and a bit frightened: you didn't waste bread. Ever.

Winifred sized up the situation. She had endured her sister's rant downstairs, known that her daughter had 'copped it,' and brought the wretched remains upstairs. She would have realised I thought I was helping.

She said, 'This will be good, Nita. We were due to make bread pudding today; I've saved some stale bread, and we've got some currants left over from the fruit cake.'

I gathered myself together. I had never been so grateful for the differences between Winifred and Anne.

I watched with relief as Mummy fetched another bowl, turned on the gas oven and found the other ingredients for the much loved Bread Pudden.

In modern day Australia, Bread and Butter custard is popular, but you never see Bread Pudding as we knew it. My mother made it again in the early days of our arrival here, probably from the same instinct of frugality that drove England, both during and after the war.

The stale and scrap bread was in the bowl; this was covered with water. After a short time, during which Mummy greased a shallow scone tray with lard and opened the pot of spice, she squeezed the water out of the soggy bread with her hands and put it into a larger bowl. It was now a firmer mass but still damp.

To this she added a heaped teaspoon of margarine by rubbing it in over the top and mixing it with her fingers. Next came a very small amount of sugar (it, too, must not be wasted) and a teaspoon of spice – mixed spice I think. No eggs of course. Lastly, in went a small handful of currants. I can see now that other ingredients might be added for interest but back then, that would have defeated the purpose of producing something very basic but very tasty.

She now needed a wooden spoon to mix it all together thoroughly. It had firmed up.

She placed globs of mixture into the greased tray and pressed with the back of the spoon until it filled evenly the scone tray. A fork scraped across the top made parallel ridges that spiked up to brown. Some mothers sprinkled sugar on top to brown it, but Mummy saved the rest of the sugar.

This went into the 'moderate' oven for 45mins (as I remember it from later Australian versions).

When the tray was removed, the top crust of the mix was browned and crisp.

Winifred cut in straight lines about two fingers' width apart the length of the tin. She then cut across the tin just over four fingers down. When cooled, the thick pieces could be lifted out, showing a light grey body and the brown crusted top. The grey didn't look attractive, but tasted very good.

Bread was saved!

I still cannot throw bread out. I'm grateful to the magpies in the front garden for putting the stale bread to good use, bringing their babies for a free feed. I understand that bread is not so good for them, but they don't score enough to worry about.

In Australia in 1951, I was fifteen when I went with my boyfriend in Wangaratta to the local Tarax Bar, the 'Milk bar and Take-away' we would call it now, and I would try hard to finish a massive chocolate milk shake he had bought me. It was too much. He kept trying to persuade me to leave it. That couldn't happen. I simply could not waste it.

As the war progressed, over the wireless and in the Daily Mirror newspaper, advice was offered as to recipes for saving foodstuffs while carefully providing nutrition. Waste must be avoided.

Each day I followed with fascination the Daily Mirror cartoon strip of cooking instructions, still now remembering drawn images of onions and other vegetables as they were cut up.

These were very realistic line drawings. Very clever.

7

SOUTH STREET MISSION 1943

Our Sunday School was at the Salvation Army Mission Centre in Hammersmith.

That title didn't mean a lot to us, we knew it as South Street Mission.

We saw people moving around, always busy. Most were in special clothes, 'uniforms' we were told but not like Daddy's or Uncle Bert's, which were Army and Navy uniforms; still, they had the word 'Army' in their title, so we thought there was some kind of connection.

They were usually called 'the Salvos'.

Ladies in the uniform wore pretty hats – bonnets. No make-up though and no sausage curls like Mummy made in her hair. Not even ringlets like Mummy did with my hair, hanging like fat sausages around my head, and a ribbon off to one side in a bow. Their hair was hidden in their bonnets.

Our Sunday School teacher was called Miss Rose; she didn't wear a bonnet or uniform. Maybe that was because she was much younger than the other ladies.

Miss Rose was kind. She gave me a bible when I left at the end of the war. I pressed rose petals in it and silver paper when I had it. She wrote in the first page of my bible: my name and the Mission's name.

Miss Rose must have thought I could remember verses fairly well, because she chose me to stand out the front of a big crowd at a special meeting, to recite the whole of, 'The Psalm of David.'

I, of course, did my usual: froze.

I knew the words, I had them in my head okay, but not one of them would come out.

Poor Miss Rose fed me the words of the psalm one line at a time:

'The Lord is my Shepherd, I shall not want,'

and I repeated it as quietly as I could. No-one could hear me.

'He maketh me to lie down in green pastures,'

This excruciating performance took its interminable time, with both of us suffering dreadfully.

Back at home I had the whole thing down pat.

I was lucky not to be strangled that day; probably by the grace of Miss Rose's non-violent religious beliefs.

'Yea, though I walk through the valley of the shadow of death,'

Well, we had some idea of that.

'Jesus bids us shine with a pure, clear light,'

We're sitting in a circle on little wooden chairs, with teacher out the front. I'm clutching my little bible card with flowers round the edge and the words, *'I will lift up mine eyes unto the hills...'*

It doesn't occur to me to think that I never saw hills to lift up mine eyes unto. Bombed-out buildings failed to lift my eyes much;- they were pretty flat, or exploded down into the ground and full of bricks and rubble. Tall houses were levelled to the pavement, you could see into some basements on the walk home from Sunday School.

'Like a little candle shining in the night,'

Well, that would be unpopular; the Air Raid Wardens would be right onto that.

Mustn't give Jerry anything to aim at.

'In this world of darkness, so we must shine,
You in your small corner, and I in mine.'

I could see how the night-light in the shelter might fit that.

'Hear the pennies dropping, listen as they fall.
Every one for Jesus, he shall have them all,'

A shiny penny in the plate for 'collection' and release from Sunday School.

The walk home with my brother.

A clear day, a clear sky, just the barrage balloons hovering fatly grey above the rooftops. No planes, either 'theirs' or 'ours' today. I'm still clutching the card I was given by the Sunday School teacher. The writing on it is a psalm that I must learn by next Sunday. I can read it by myself of course, I'm seven. I've had two years at school already. I can read better than my brother. He says I'm just guessing the words. He gets annoyed because I keep getting moved up into his class. He's eight and a half, but he doesn't pay attention in class. I pay attention to everything, otherwise things can go wrong without me seeing it coming. I watch everything. Everybody. Including my brother. Especially my brother.

He's telling me to hurry up. Why? What's it matter?

'Hello little girl, what's your name?'

'Nita? That's pretty. I'm John. I've got some pennies here, shiny ones. Would you like two? You can have them if you like; and two for your brother. Look at that. Hold them tight, you don't want to lose them.'

I stop walking and look at the pennies. It's true, they're copper and very shiny. The man must have polished them. Why? To give to children? That's kind.

There aren't many men around these days; not like my Daddy's age, usually very old like Grandad; or boys like Tony my brother.

This man is wearing grubby white overalls, so maybe he has a job that is an 'essential service' like Mummy in the Post Office. Mummy wears clean clothes.

'Come ON Nita!'

'Oh, that's alright Nita, no hurry there. We can go for a different walk if you like.' Have you got your pennies safe?

'You can hold my hand.'

I was used to obeying grown-ups, even strangers; there were consequences if I didn't. I had experience of that in Penzance.

During the raids, grown-ups would guide you to an air raid shelter if you weren't home.

This wasn't an air raid though.

'I'm not allowed in bomb sites. Where's my brother?'

Of course he's gone. Tony could leave me cold at any time and go about his own interests. Still, he disappeared very quickly.

'Don't worry about him. I expect he wants to put his pennies in his money box. You can do that too. Later.'

There were steps down, very dusty, all covered with broken bricks and slate. Not dark though, because there was nearly no ceiling. Rubbish and rubble and wood everywhere, just like Glasgow after the bomb. There was no house up above of course and the walls that were there were all broken and fallen outward, but there was still a sort of a room.

I stood still, watching.

The man was not close, I could look at him. He knew that; he wanted that.

When he could be sure I was really looking, he opened his overall and took his thing out. I didn't know what that was called. My mother called my brother's thing a 'daddle', but it was little and white and wobbly like a worm.

I looked at the man's thing. You couldn't call it a 'daddle'. It was big and straight and sort of darker.

'You can touch it if you like.'

I stayed still. Watching.

The man, John, came close and squatted in front of me. I didn't like him. I didn't like his face.

He was different. He looked different, he said different things in a different voice. I watched his eyes. His eyes were different, his smile was supposed to be friendly.

He reached out with both hands and took my knickers down; they were around my ankles.

He touched me in a different way, where no-one touched me.

I stood still, watching his eyes.

He rubbed me down there with one finger; side to side, side to side, watching my face.

He kept going. I didn't like it. I didn't like him. He kept going, watching my face. I hated that.

My knickers were down around my ankles. I couldn't move. I couldn't get them up.

He kept going, looking into my eyes. I was trapped.

A sound outside!

Another.

Boots scraping.

'NITA!!'

He jumped up, running, tripping, doing up his overalls as he ran – out the back way through the mess and rubble. Gone.

I stood.

Then I ran; I pulled up my knickers, then shot up the cement steps, out into the bright sunlight, straight into legs, legs in sailor trousers, legs I threw myself at; grabbed, 'DADDY!'

No, It was not Daddy; it was a very young sailor boy in uniform, shocked to the bone after helping the search.

Tony my brother had rushed home to report the abduction. He was absolutely responsible for my timely rescue. If he never did another thing for me it would be enough.

There was a gathering of searchers, called in from the passers-by as Tony brought a panicked Winifred to the approximate scene of the crime.

My mother held me against her, crying. She didn't drop down to my level or look at my face. She didn't ask me if I was alright; she just crushed me to her and wept.

In my dazed state I had a feeling: 'She's crying for herself, not me.'

How could I, at only seven years old, comprehend the emotions screaming through her mind and body.

I felt only my own alienation.

This reaction continued to predominate throughout the aftermath of the event as the police tried to follow up with their questions.

At seven years old, I regarded a policewoman across the dining room table she employed as a desk. I might as well have been surveying her across the width of London. My mother (not feeling like 'Mummy' at this time) stood stiffly far to my left in silence. She seemed as troubled as I was about the policewoman's presence.

The police woman asked me, a seven year old, to tell them, 'What happened? What did the man do?'

I stood alone in the centre of the room, weighing up the situation, trying to see my way out and, as was my usual practice, becoming passive; still; thinking.

Again as usual, I took the child's way out. To each question I answered: 'Nothing.'

What I could not face was the prospect of the drama I sensed would have to ensue, even if I had the words then to relate the (incomprehensible) details.

I had information that they could have used, but of which they had no conception.

My visual memory was developing well. I could have told them then what 'John' looked like and what he was wearing. Even now, I could draw him fairly accurately. Why would I not remember?

I was not interrogated again.

As a child, I had no wish to confront the consequences of 'telling all.' I can understand perfectly the silence of others who have taken that line.

Nowadays, adult women and even young girls and boys, do have the words for what has happened to them, but they also fear the reaction of either the authorities or even their loved-ones.

Rather than criticise their late reporting, why not congratulate them on summoning up their courage at last and for joining the voices of other brave victims.

There are other evils in the world than war.

As I left the room after the excruciating interview, I bumped into my brother and cousin, who were pressed to the door trying to follow the, to them, Soap Opera.

Of course they asked me, 'What did the man do to you?'

I answered with a throwaway: 'He pulled down my pants and showed me his.'

No, of course, they didn't believe me.

I never told again.

I have been debating with myself, back and forth, for and against, the inclusion of this story in 'The Kite Makers.'

Is it relevant? Do people need to know this? Will it seem exhibitionist? Attention seeking? In bad taste? Or worse, self pitying.

Will anyone pay attention to it? Will I be believed?

Is it pertinent? It did occur during the war in Britain. This man's presence in London was exceptional for his age group, about thirty-thirty-five as I visualise him now. Was he, for some reason, rejected by the armed forces?

Today I witnessed on the television news and again in the Sunday paper, comments from journalists, movie stars, producers and other people of varied public visibility, many expressions of disgust at the reported (alleged) harassment and/or sexual assault/rape of women over many years, perpetrated (allegedly) by a prominent Hollywood personality.

How many times must I use the word 'allegedly'?

The women who have been speaking up in recent weeks have been applauded for their courage by a vast majority. A vocal minority have protested that, after all, they might have reported these issues when an incident occurred. How come they're speaking up now?

Well, why not do the usual? Mark the victim as the villain, the weakling, the liar?

I was seven years old when I first experienced sexual assault and that was by no means the last. Most pretty little girls and attractive teenagers have their stories. Too many boys have theirs as well. We didn't even have to be particularly attractive.

I now report that not once did I tell the people around me what had happened on any of those occasions. Not once.

In the lines above I have put forward possible explanations for this reticence.

Even now it gives me pause.

Embroidery

Mummy had bought me some 'transfers' - paper sheets with special drawings on them, thin blue lines but not coloured in.

You placed the paper on a bit of cotton material and ironed it. This made the drawing go over to the cotton material. Mummy had bought me some coloured 'embroidery silks.' She threaded a needle for me so that I could sew around on the blue lines. It took a little while, but I learnt to make a line with 'back stitch'. Later she showed me how to do 'chain stitch.'

This was a whole new world.

It was a bit annoying that I couldn't thread the needle each time and had to ask her to do it for me, even more embarrassing when I had to ask her in front of the ladies she had visiting. They thought I was SO SWEET.

She would only thread a short length at a time, 'That's long enough for a little girl.'

Humiliating.

I just had to practice and practice till I could do it all by myself!

Transfer embroideries could be used to decorate handkerchiefs, but I could not be trusted with those.

If I managed not to lose my hankie at school, I ruined it
anyway by chewing and tearing a corner with my teeth. This was
a nervous habit adopted when my mother stopped me sucking
my thumb. She sent me to school with twelve-inch squares of
old sheeting fabric which I could chew all I liked, till she put a
stop to that and I started biting my nails instead. My teeth
survived the thumb sucking and my finger nails have not been
ruined. I never transferred my oral fixation to smoking cigarettes. Then again, I do have a healthy enthusiasm for chocolate.

Our mother couldn't watch us all the time. The 'helicopter
parenting' of the new millennium, the constant and anxious
supervision of offspring, was yet to come and quite impossible
for wartime mothers.

One would think, also, that daily reminders of impending
death by bombing would eliminate an urge for children to take
risks. But children feel a need in their bones to take risks; they
test the limits, they constantly affirm their own survival potential. Just like kittens really.

Out of sight of parents who might caution them 'not to go
to the marsh' or 'the river', or not to play with 'those rough children', 'mess with fireworks' or speak to strangers, they will have a
go at the very things that they know are taboo.

Connie and Tony had a new idea one day when both
mothers were elsewhere. We were all on the balcony of the First
Floor, looking over at the concrete 'area'. In no time at all a challenge presented itself.

'We can climb down the drainpipe. It's just there, next to the
railing.'

The downpipe ran down the wall from the roof guttering,
passing between the front door and the end of the balcony.

'I'll go first.' Tony of course.

He eased over the balcony railing holding tightly as he stretched his left leg across to the drainpipe. One hand followed, with Tony spread-eagled between rail and pipe. He managed to get his right hand and leg across, clung, then half slid and half climbed down to the concrete of the ground below. None of this was witnessed by a soul in the street, otherwise a stop would have been put to it.

I was next. Connie watched. Tony egged me on.

Boys of that era wore short trousers, good serviceable socks and plain, sensible shoes.

Little girls wore skirts or dresses, little white socks with pretty edges and patent leather button-up shoes. Not for mountain climbing. Until quite recently I have had a very strong body which has obeyed me. It must be genetic, because I have never been athletic.

Somehow I managed to live. Connie must have had severe doubts about this possibility by now, because she disappeared inside. Boys didn't think girls were brave anyway, so I don't suppose she lost much 'face'.

I went back to my plasticene cats. I continued to review my opinion about Tony's and Connie's judgement and the wisdom of copying them.

Scarlet Fever

We were in the sitting room in the house we still shared with Auntie Anne: Mummy, Tony and I.

We usually ate in the upstairs kitchen, in our place at the very top of the house. The sitting room was one level down. We might have been eating there to be near the fire. The weather was getting cold.

It was raining out. This was good, because the more cloud there was, the less likely the Germans were to come bombing. Anyway, it was daytime. They usually came at night. Not always.

I was supposed to be eating my lunch: pea soup. I liked that, but today I couldn't even look at it.

I really didn't want to eat.

Tony was well into his. We both always devoured what was put in front of us willingly, if not enthusiastically in some instances. We were usually hungry and took what we could.

'Eat your soup Nita.'

'I can't, Mummy. I don't want it.' I started crying. I was suddenly very sad.

She moved fast out of her chair, taking me with her to the fire. Amazingly, she lifted my jumper, looking at my tummy!

What ever she was looking for did not please her. I was rushed upstairs to the big double bed, into my nightie and between the sheets.

Dr. Stein arrived. A fight ensued during which he tried to get a tongue depressor into my mouth. I was having none of that. I knew children who had had their tonsils taken out. He wasn't getting my tonsils, whatever they were!

Dr. Stein finished with me and disappeared, murmuring quietly to my mother on his way out.

Some people arrived acting very important and managing. They wore white coats.

I was still crying, but quietly now. Dr Stein never did get that thing in my mouth.

I was carried out to an ambulance with a nurse and every-thing! This was amazing! I stopped snuffling. We were going somewhere. But not Mummy. Why not Mummy?

The nurse asked me my name.

'Anita Baker.' I though she might want the whole thing. She had on a blue uniform and looked special.

'Hallo Anita, my name's Nurse O'Brien. I'm coming on the ride with you. This is called an ambulance.'

I knew that from the newspaper. I read Mummy's newspaper every morning, especially 'Garth' and 'Jane.'

I was on a bed in the ambulance – in my nightie still. I never went out in my nightie; well, not unless there was bombing and we had to get out to the shelter. Then Mummy was there of course.

Where could we possibly be going?

'Can I look out the window, please?'

'Oh, I think you're too small, dear'. She was saying that to distract me from my strange situation, but that was fine; I was willing to be distracted. I got up on my knees.

'I can see alright. I'm big enough to reach.'

'Well, so you are. You're bigger than I thought. How old are you then?'

'I'm seven. I go to school. Why isn't Mummy coming?'

I could see the streets of London going by. I had been on a double-decker bus before, but not in an ordinary car. This wasn't an ordinary car really. Why am I here? Where are we going?

'Your Mummy had to stay home today. Where we're going is for children; sick children. You know that you're not well, do you? There will be other children there that are not well.'

That was no attraction for me. 'Other children', especially strange children, usually meant trouble.

I knew something was wrong with me. I had a rash all over my tummy. It was that that had upset Mummy so much. I had Scarlet Fever.

Our arrival at the hospital meant a bustle of activity in which I was moved out of the ambulance and carried by a man in a white coat into a huge building. I was put on a chair in an office with big people all around. I started to cry again.

At first everyone ignored me. They all had blue uniforms. The office was small. It belonged to a lady named Matron. I was scared stiff of her. On her head she wore what looked like a white pillow-case all stiff and folded and sticking out in triangles at the sides. This was how you knew she was Matron. The nurses had little caps, white and stiff but quite small. And most were younger than Matron. And a lot thinner.

Matron turned her sights on me.

'See that strap on the wall? Stop that crying NOW or I will use it!'

She turned away, quite assured of the effect of that.

I gagged and stopped breathing, terrified in case a sound should leave my mouth. No doubt some whimpering escaped, but Matron's attention was on important organisational matters: which bed I was to occupy for starters.

The wards were overcrowded as it was. The Scarlet Fever epidemic was killing children. The war wounded were filling the hospital.

I don't know now which County we were in. I don't remember any bombing during my stay, but the ambulance journey had not been so very long. That doesn't mean there was no bombing necessarily; bombing had become commonplace, and the hospital had no air-raid practices or procedures, so life just went on. And things were happening close to me of much more dramatic import, or so it seemed to me.

For a while I was too sick to care.

I was aware of the row of beds nearby, occupied by other sick children, but more immediate was the management I received from the nurses.

This was nothing like home; nurses were nothing like Mummy. Some were kind like Mummy, some were cross like Auntie Anne. Why people liked me or disliked me I could not tell. It did seem that way. I sometimes felt it was because I talked 'nicely'. My mother insisted on talking nicely.

She had an accent I now know, as I did: London. But London has more than one accent: Cockney, for instance – within the sound of Bow Bells, Bow being the church. Our accent was Hammersmith. Even now in Australia, the occasional person takes exception to the traces of Hammersmith in my speech.

The hospital nurses brought me food that at first I didn't want; they washed me, brushing my wet hair flat against my head and eliminating the ringlets that my mother cultivated so diligently. They made my bed with me in it. They brought me bed pans and embarrassed me by examining my output and discussing it between themselves.

Endless time passed. My health improved.

'You have a parcel, Nita; from your Mummy.'

Mummy! I hadn't seen Mummy for ages. I took the package with trembling hands. Other children watched with unconcealed envy and resentment as I accepted my treasure.

I tore away the string and brown paper to find a box inside. There was an apple! And drawing paper! And a long, new pencil! Just for me. I cried with relief. Mummy had not forgotten me.

There were probably other things in the box, probably a letter, but the important items stay etched in my memory. An apple. Drawing things.

I finally remembered to say 'Thank you' to the nurse, who seemed interested in my parcel, but maybe she was just being nice. I can call her, 'Nurse Smith', but I don't really remember her name, just what she looked like. I'm still like that: faces, yes. Names, not so good. What I thought of them has been remembered well with each face.

Nurse Smith was lovely to me. Maybe she favoured me. I think so. I think maybe that's why Nurse Heinz didn't like me. I remember her name, with good reason. Maybe she thought I was being spoilt. That's something that happened from time to time; it started with Auntie Anne. And Tony. And Connie.

Nurse Heinz snatched away the brown paper and string, probably to fold and use again. Paper and string were not wasted.

'What have you got, Nita?' The girl in the next bed was trying to see, but lost interest when I held up my drawing things. She didn't imagine I'd share the apple.

The Scarlet Fever must have been getting better. I was interested in food again. An item that I had not met before, nor indeed later, was a cup of warm 'broth' we were all given at bed time – that is, the time to settle down to sleep. This broth, as I can only surmise, was made with potato, barley or some soft grain, sago and salt and pepper. I may not have that exactly right, and there were likely to be other ingredients, but I still remember the taste and texture. It was indeed pleasantly settling.

During the mornings I was now allowed out of bed with other children, in my nightie, dressing gown and slippers. We were told not to go near 'the men.'

'The men' were wounded servicemen who would sit in the paved area outside the glass doors of our ward. Some were in wheel chairs with rugs over their knees. All were injured. We didn't know what that meant in detail, only that they had been hurt in the war.

Of course we went to talk to them. How long since we had seen Daddy?

The men wanted to talk to us. They had not seen their children, those that were old enough to have them. Many were much too young as I saw it.

As their conditions improved the men were allowed outside visitors. This was strictly limited, as the nurses were overworked. No doubt Matron was running a tight ship. We were contagious and allowed no visitors at all. Matron may well have wanted to keep our germs away from the injured men.

Time passed.

'You can have dinner at the table now, Nita, with the other children.'

A long table was set up not far from the fireplace. A plate of food arrived in front of each of us. This was wonderful: to sit up and eat properly!

Nurse Smith, Nurse Heinz and some other nurses stood between our table and the fire. I was only vaguely aware of them, focused on my dinner. My back was to them.

'I like Nurse Smith best, she's nice,' said Sally, smiling

smugly at her neighbour, fully aware of Nurse Smith within earshot.

'I like Nurse Johnson,' said Gracie, likewise. There can always be points to win.

'I like Nurse Heinz,' said little Johnny, who didn't have a clue.

This was too much for me!

'I hate Nurse Heinz!,' I cried, 'She's crabby!'

My plate disappeared. Nurse Heinz snatched it away and stood glowering at me.

'That's it! You can forget dinner, you nasty little girl! You have no gratitude for what you get. You're a spoilt little girl!'

I burst into tears, not only afraid of her anger, but appalled that my meal was gone. Each meal was precious. We had none to spare. I dissolved. She was much too powerful.

Perhaps the other nurses broke in and spoke to Nurse Heinz, I don't know, but she put my plate back in front of me. To this day the word 'dinner' has special weight to it if linked with the idea of deprivation. Even the idea of my dog missing out on her 'dinner' can make my stomach clench.

I forced what I could down my neck, not wanting to appear ungrateful, but no longer able to eat. The other children stared at me in between mouthfuls. I had committed a felony; they hoped to avoid that.

I had been stupid, too silly to check who was behind us hearing our talk, and the truth was still important to me. To hear Nurse Heinz praised was unbearable and I became careless.

Only in writing this story has it occurred to me that Nurse Heinz might have had her own traumas. Was she German? Was she Jewish or of some group not acceptable to Hitler? Was she new in England? Where was her family?

Dr Stein in Hammersmith? Was he recently arrived in England, or a long time resident? As a child these names had no significance for me. My mother called him Doctor Steen.

Nurse Heinz may have had miseries quite specific to her.

• • •

My Scarlet Fever was gone. I now had Chicken Pox caught from the other children.

This was hell. I was told not to scratch, but of course I did and still carry scars as evidence.

As my health improved I was moved to a bed a little further away from the nurses' station. There was a boy in the next bed about my age.

We were nearly caught one night giggling as we showed each other our bare tummies. Who knows how far that might have gone if Nurse hadn't run up, thinking she heard crying.

After a total of seven weeks I was allowed home. Mummy fixed my hair: I was back in ringlets with a ribbon on one side of my head.

I returned to school to find that the girls were all skipping with ropes. I couldn't do it. I was out of touch. Everyone had new friends.

My teacher had changed; I was no longer with Miss King, whom I adored. My heart was broken. I didn't want to go to school.

Miss King had liked me too; she took me home one weekend with another girl, but that girl had cried for her mother all night in the double bed beside me. Next time, Miss King took me home on my own.

Mummy was still letting people borrow me, possibly to get me out of the bombing from time to time. Nobody seemed to want to borrow Tony.

Miss King liked acting. She was in a play called 'The Red Suite', a drama, very exciting. Mummy and I nearly didn't make it to the performance. The piece of paper we had with the directions had St Pancras Station on one side and Paddington on the other. We went to the wrong one at first. Big panic until we worked it out.

I remember the stage lighting for the 'Red' room; very scary.

I was so proud of Miss King.

Like it or not, I had to go to school. I had to have a new teacher.

One change after another; nothing to be done about it.

Hammersmith Bridge

'Don't go near the river, Okay?'

Auntie Anne dished out orders a lot, but some of them didn't make sense, so they stood a good chance of being ignored. What could the river do?

Mummy was at work and I was stuck with Tony and Connie, who were stuck with me and showed it.

'No, no. We won't. We'll go down Bridge Avenue to the bridge, but we won't go down the embankment steps. No.' Connie was reassuring.

'Can we go on the bridge, Auntie?' Tony was exploring boundaries.

'Well.... I suppose you can, but no climbing on the railing. If you fall in the Thames you'll die. That'll be the last of you.' Was there a glimpse of malice there?' Of course not.

We were immortal anyway. The bombs never got us, did they? The cliffs in Cornwall failed in the attempt. The river was nothing. The Thames was usually smooth and peaceful, not like the Cornish sea, smashing around like billyo. The boats on the river were an endless source of entertainment for London children – and at Oxford and Cambridge boat race time, for adults as well.

Hammersmith Bridge was a magnet for us. I was trusted to wheel my dolly's pram over it and back, even on my own. There were few dangers for children in the streets then; adults didn't disturb you, they had too much to do to bother with kids. They always helped when there was an Air Raid siren if you weren't near a shelter you knew. Once when I was watching a boat race there was a bit of a worry, a strange man had said, 'Hello Nita' in a creepy way. He must have heard my brother use my name. I moved away from him. There were lots of other adults around that day and he disappeared.

Connie and Tony led the march to the bridge. I kept up as best I could. I preferred to be a bit separate from them anyway. They would have loved to lose me but knew it was more than their lives were worth.

On the bridge. A really good view. The bridge itself was well known to us with its huge towers and sweeping cables. Its railings were iron and filled with a diamond pattern of thin, flat bars. It joined Hammersmith to the other part of London, a part we never went to. It was important, just like the other bridges over the Thames and as such was a coveted target for German bombers.

No climbing. So, once you've taken in the river and the boats, not much to do.

The sky was mostly blue, so people were out. Still, there wasn't much to do.

The walk along the Embankment looked good. People were down there walking.

'What's wrong with the walk?' Tony reckoned we could go there.

I held back. The other two headed to the Embankment that had served the city for centuries with steps to the water that were showing wear, dipping in the middle and rounded at the front edge. If they were wet, you could slip.

Tony and Connie were well ahead now, oblivious as to my absence. They were studying a set of steps from the Embankment that ran at right angles right down into and under the water. How many boots had brought merchandise up those steps from the barges and boats?

I was still close to the bridge. There was an identical set of steps right by me; much safer looking than the cliff at Penzance.

Now Tony was sitting half way down the steps. Connie was

considering joining him. They were not near me, but I could work out what was going on.

I looked at my steps.

Tentatively I placed my feet on the first, then the second step. I sat.

The river moved peacefully by, except for swiftly swirling currents around the base of the bridge pylons nearby to my left. That might be dangerous.

I sat, taking it in.

I edged down one step on my bottom. And some more.

In the water!

Without warning I had slipped on the wet seaweed splashed by the tide on the lower steps. I was fully under the water.

An instinct that I had no idea about caused me to roll over and face the submerged steps. They still exist as an image in my mind. I had opened my eyes. I clawed towards the slimy green steps, pushing back the water with my hands. I had never learned to swim: it was wartime London.

When, in Australia, optimists tried to teach me to swim, I always got to a certain stage, then stopped. Water, being submerged in it, holds no charms for me. Australians can hardly understand that. They start to play with water soon after birth.

Water was not for playing.

I somehow managed to pull myself out. No-one was watching; it was all over in a moment.

I mounted the steps, crying, drenched to the skin, an object of amusement for a boy and girl, arms around each other at the top of the steps. You can bet they couldn't swim either, but thought the sight of me looking like a drowned rat was hilarious. Neither one of them would have or could have saved me.

Very soon they would be serving in the war.

I cried all the way home. Connie and Tony were nowhere to be seen.

Auntie Anne had my little two-piece summer suit on the line when Mummy got home.

Need I describe the scene that followed?

8

MALVERN 1944

'Heil Hitler! Heil Hitler!'

Tony was strutting around the road with our cousins, goose-stepping and holding a finger across under his nose for a tooth-brush moustache and with the Nazi salute stiffened diagonally up in the air. Hilarious!

Hitler's name was well known to us now, and ridiculing him was a much applauded sport in all circles.

Airmen sang:

> *'Hitler has only got one ball.*
> *Goering has two but rather small.*
> *Himmler has something simmler,*
> *And poor old Goebbels has no balls at all.'*

Humour was an important part of the War Effort.

Arthur Askey and Flanagan and Allen featured with gentle jollity on the wireless.

'Making the best of each day'.
'Underneath the arches' and
'Nice people, with nice manners, but not much
    money at all.
Nice habits, they keep rabbits, but not much money
    at all.'

Rabbits were kept now as a future source of meat protein.
Auntie Anne had 'Whiskers' in London.
Gracie Fields made everyone laugh:

> *'Everyone's pinching my butter.*
> *They won't leave my butter alone.'*

George Formby was very popular singing his father's original
songs:

> *'I love to go swimmin' with wimmin' and*
> *'When I'm cleaning windows.'*

Things he was seeing. Very naughty.
By contrast, Vera Lynn tore heart strings with

> *'There'll be bluebirds over the white cliffs of Dover -*
> *'The shepherds will tend their sheep, the valley will*
>   *bloom again,*
> *And Jimmy will go to sleep in his own little room*
>   *again.'*

Jimmy, Johnny and Tom perhaps now sleep somewhere in a
field in France.

> *'We'll meet again, don't know where, don't know*
>   *when.'*

Perhaps these songs didn't rate with Beethoven's *'Song of Joy'*, but playing German music was frowned upon by the Government. You might be tempted to admire the enemy.

Nevertheless, *'Lily Marlene,'* was translated and sung. Marlene Dietrich carried the crown with that one.

Churchill at first tried to protect the troops from musical entertainment, thinking it would 'soften' them. He came to realise how badly its therapeutic value was needed, and sent artists to war zones to lift troubled spirits.

In London, a series of shows called, *'Every Night Something Different,'* was more often referred to as, *'Every Night Something Awful,'* ENSA. The real talent was going elsewhere.

The war songs affect me now more than they seemed to then with my limited understanding. Yet I remember them well, including all the words, so they were getting through at some level. Now, in my eighties, I can be brought close to tears by a first line.

'Socials' still occurred in the working class communities. Dances were held at which American airmen from the nearby aerodrome were appearing.

We were in Malvern, Worcestershire, near the Welsh border. We were visiting Auntie Vi, our father's sister.

Auntie Vi had nine sons; she had been 'trying for a girl.' That never happened, but Uncle Sid, according to our mother, couldn't keep it in his pants anyway. Auntie Vi looked worn out so Uncle Sid was turning his attentions to Winifred, who gave him short shrift. He was a 'masher.'

Why was he not at the war?

Cousins Doug, John, Geoff and more than I can remember, showed us around Malvern. As city kids we were not acquainted with the likes of the Malvern Hills, haystacks and horses.

The cousins were acquainted with American airmen. They had soon learned to follow them around and pester them with: 'Got any gum chum?' The airmen always gave it out. Tony and I joined in that game, enjoying the flat mint-flavoured

strips wrapped in their silver paper. Once we even scored
chocolate!

The aerodrome was very close by, so close that we would
throw ourselves on the concrete road whenever a massive Flying
Fortress took off so close above.

The 'yanks' provided another diversion for kids.

After a morning of rolling down one of the smaller slopes
near town – and getting black and blue in the process – we
would roam the grassy area at the base of the hill searching for
'balloons.' We knew the Yanks and their girlfriends left them
behind. I don't believe the older cousins knew what they really
were, since they joined in the activity.

The 'balloons' were found in the grass: flat circles of whitish thin rubber with a thin round outside edge and crumpled thin rubber filling in between. The whole thing was, say, one and a half inches across.

They had been used.

They were dry.

We worked hard at blowing them up.

They weren't much as balloons go, but it was the searching and finding that was the game.

My brother had taken part in another 'game' with two of the younger cousins.

We had just been chased out of a field by a beautiful black horse, who may well have believed we were there to feed him some treat. He came speeding after us as, panicking, we fled to the whitethorn hedge and out over the wooden stile.

I ran home.

Tony, Geoff and Jim found a safer field with a promising haystack in it.

The boys had matches: Geoff was already smoking in secret.

Later, for children's ears only, they described with extravagant imagery the conflagration that they had created.

In 1949, in Australia, my brother ignited two fires near Wangaratta, Victoria, in the deadly dangerous bushfire season.

Tony, Geoff and Jim had never been caught by the adults for the haystack fire. A die was cast.

The Tea room

Mummy and I were wandering around the shopping street; we were wearing pretty cotton dresses and sandals, just like being on a seaside holiday.

'Nita, we'll have a cup of tea in here, and some scones.'

Mummy wanted to show me some paintings on the tearoom walls. She said a real artist had done them; she thought I'd like to see them.

'It's very well done,' she said.

'What are the ladies doing?' I asked. 'And why aren't they wearing much?'

Mummy always knew; although often the answer didn't help.

'Artists always do that, leave the clothes off. That's ART.' She said.

'Oh! Like 'Jane' in the paper?' A popular cartoon strip.

'Well, not exactly, dear.' She paused for a moment, sorting out the differences in her mind.

Winifred, the arithmetic whiz, had not an artistic bone in her body, but wanted to feed the tendency growing in me. I thought also that the tea, scones, jam and cream pulled her in here at least as strongly as the art. No doubt she, like me, appreciated the different diet available in some country towns.

The weather was fine, so Mummy took us out into the Tea Garden to sit on the grass.

An American airman came up to say hello.

Mummy didn't like that, even though he knew her name.

'Hi Win, great to see you here. That your little girl is it? Very pretty.' I was used to that.

Mummy was not happy.

'I'll get you some more biscuits,' said the airman. He was looking at the remains of the scones.

They're scones, not 'biscuits'. Americans are funny.

'Back in a sec.'

Mummy moved fast. Our tea, what was left of it, was deserted on the spot and we were out of there. Hardly time to brush the grass off our skirts.

Winifred, with her love of dancing, must have attended a 'social' organised for the airmen. Auntie Vi wouldn't have gone with her, she was always too tired and anyway, Uncle Sid wouldn't have had that!

A lady down the road went with Winifred, all dressed up and laughing at the prospect. It felt quite adventurous and even a little wicked, married women planning to dance with total strangers. Let alone American airmen!

Winifred very much enjoyed dancing with the servicemen, but had no desire to provide other benefits.

Now she did not wish me to get the wrong impression.

I was innocent of any imagination in that area; indeed, quite uninformed about anything adults – some adults – might get up to.

We managed to lose the airman. I felt sorry about that, it seemed a bit unkind.

Scrumping

I had to go to school on weekdays in Malvern. I was eight years old at that time and had already attended other schools; this was my third.

I was becoming adept at coping with change – change of school, change of home, change of friends. In Malvern the school offered me what 'home' lacked: girls to play with (Connie didn't count).

My Malvern cousins, the Underhills, were all boys. Most of their games were 'boy' games by my observations. I think now that the boys were just rough, behaviour sanctioned by adults with, 'Well, boys will be boys.' Nevertheless, I played along, becoming quite proficient at soccer and cricket. And stealing.

I didn't see the girls from school at the weekend, so followed around with the boys.

I learned what 'Scrumping' meant. Its correct application was to apples and the pinching of.

'Scrumpy,' was stewed apple.

The boys, not sticklers for terminology, applied the name to the stealing of any fruit.

The boys threw around another new expression, 'Wizard Prang!' which meant 'good' or 'very good'. It had originated with British airmen. It made as much sense as the more recent,

'Wicked!' or 'Fully Sick!' which will be out of fashion before you read this.

We marched off to a scrumping target several streets away: a plum tree hanging well over a garden wall.

This was a 'blood plum' tree, with dark red leaves hiding a special delicacy; once again a treat not available in London. This purple, nearly black fat fruit, when bitten into showed golden and juicy beyond measure. Those plums were large and shiny, hard until you bit into them, then shocking you by squirting juice everywhere. Our clothes must have told the parents what we had been up to, but not a word was said.

Boys will be boys.

The Country Fair

'Nita, get down from there!'

I was sitting up high on a concrete block building. It had no windows, just a heavy locked door. We didn't know what it was for, but we could get up and sit on its flat concrete roof. It wasn't very high.

I was busy manufacturing whistles. The cousins had shown me how.

You take a hard almond shell after the green fleshy cover is off, then you rub one end on the concrete roof till you've worn it through. You repeat this at the other end. If the holes at each end are the right size you have a whistle. The almond inside is the 'pea' that makes the sound when you blow into it.

My cousins had also shown me how to make a 'conker.' This was a horse chestnut threaded on a string. The horse chestnut was selected for size and potential hardness. A hole was bored through its centre, from top to bottom. The string was threaded through and left with a substantial 'tail.' A knot at the other end prevented the string from pulling through and out.

The game, competition, was played by taking turns in holding your conker string with the conker itself dangling on the end. Your opponent held their 'weapon' – conker – on the knuckle of one hand with the string going between two fingers. Their other hand held the string very taut below until great tension was achieved, then let the conker fly out at speed and hit your conker. Your conker might split. If it didn't, you would now attack the other conker in the same way. A successful (surviving) conker might become a 'oner' or a 'twoer', depending on how many other conkers it had smashed.

My whistle was not quite as ferocious a device as that.

My next job was to make a bubble pipe out of an acorn and a straw. I was too busy to bother with Doug.

'Nita! You'll miss the fun. We're all going to the green; there's a fair on the green. It turned up last night!'

Oh....

'Get your pocket money; we can get fairy floss if we're lucky. Or toffee apples, maybe.'

What's a toffee apple? Or fairy floss?

Better check.

I climbed down with my bits of almond, acorn and straw. Doug was rattling on about the fair. I had no idea what it was all about. 'Fairs' didn't happen in Hammersmith.

We went by the house to lay our hands on what money we could. I had six whole shillings of pocket money – a fortune. Doug looked at it with something like hunger.

Some of our other cousins joined us. Tony was off somewhere with one of the others, scrumping. We trouped through the town to the green, all flushed with excitement and pocket money. The unlucky ones had already spent theirs. Tony and I got more than they did, but then Mummy didn't have nine of us.

The music hit us first; a cacophony of sound from many sources, most dominant the melody from the calliope within the merry-go-round; as we came nearer, voices could be discerned, raised to advertise special treats and exciting attractions.

We raced into the confusion of people and things: tents,

booths, stages with people yelling their lungs out, caravans and animals, flags and banners everywhere.

We passed an organ grinder with his monkey on a chain. the little animal darted everywhere he could on and around the man, holding a metal cup that he offered to people in the hope of a few pennies.

We couldn't find fairy floss anywhere. Perhaps rationing had something to do with that. A gypsy lady had toffee apples. I heard the words 'black market' sometimes at home, it wasn't allowed, but things like ordinary sugar could sometimes be found.

I looked up.

In the sky above me were people flying!

They were riding in a flying boat! Memories of kites and my special seagull in Cornwall took me up in the sky to ride with those lucky people.

The flying boat was indeed boat shaped, but it was gaily painted in reds, blues, yellows and greens. How I wanted to do that: sit in one of those boats and fly, FLY!

Doug said, 'That's OK, you can do that. You have the money. Plenty. We can manage with what we have.'

Those who had money, counted it and found they could afford a ticket. I had more.

We paid and waited our turn, myself nearly faint with excitement.

Flying. Sailing through the air in our boat. Leaning back with my face tipped skyward. Flying over the whole world!

The boat was my seagull just like in Cornwall. I was a fairy! Flying!

The ride stopped all too soon.

We offloaded and tumbled into the mainstream of people. The

cousins had run out of money, but I still had some. I wasn't going anywhere now. They could do what they liked. I had only one use for my money.

I bought another ticket as the boys left me to see other spectacles. I was old enough at eight years to stay on my own. I flew again.

And again.

I headed home half drunk from the experience but by no means sated.

I needed money.

I had to ride again before the fair moved on. It might never come again. We might go back to the city, where there were no fairs, no flying boats. Just sirens and bombs.

Our room was empty. The adults were out. The drawer that always held our pocket money was next to the double bed. Mine was gone of course; spent. Tony's was still there. He was out.

Money. Enough for three rides.

Not mine.

Who would know?

I sat, knowing right from wrong. You didn't lie, you didn't steal.

I was flying for the last time up in the sky, up above the world, far from the ground and its unending troubles; far from thoughts of bombing, evacuation and grief for a long lost father, all these thoughts that dragged in the back of my mind, rooting me to the earth.

The flying boat took me again into the new and perfect world of the open sky.

Below.

I looked down. My brother Tony was there, crying, calling out my name. Reaching his hands towards me, pleading.

'Where did you get all the money? Where is my pocket money?'

The cousins had told him where I had gone, what I was doing. He knew well enough where his money had gone.

I felt sick. The ride thankfully ended; it was no longer a joy.

"Don't lie to me! You've spent your money, haven't you? Stop lying.'

Mummy was going for Tony, knowing full well his ways. This was just more of the same. Just like him: lying and cheating.

I stood mute; paralysed, terrified.

I had never done anything like this before. What will happen now if I tell the truth?

My brother was weeping bitterly. For once he was innocent. For once he knew I had committed a crime.

'Nita took it. She took it to spend at the fair.'

'Don't lie!'

Mummy had had enough of him. She left the room. I hurried after her, quite unable to face Tony's pain.

That I had caused.

In Malvern, a burning haystack had brought Tony great joy since he was never held accountable and had no conscience where punishment was not involved. He never showed moral judgement of his own. The pain he gave the farmer would be unfelt by him. He could do it again.

In Malvern, I lied and stole and was not caught by any adult, but the pain I had caused was intense, immediate and in my face. I cannot see a flying boat even now without sadness and shame.

I do not steal.

I find even polite 'white lies' quite difficult and will avoid them.

9

BACK IN LONDON

The whole class was struggling with a new skill - knitting: purl and plain, or just plain if you weren't so good at it.

The boys were not offended at what might have been called 'girls' work' in another time. They knew the sailors were knitting their own socks on board ship, and darning and sewing on buttons.

Traditional 'men's' work was being carried out by women all over Britain.

Gender stereotypes were severely dented if not eradicated.

We were knitting squares for patchwork blankets for the soldiers. We were given coloured wool contributed to the school by those that could spare it. Old jumpers were being unravelled for the wool. The sense of doing something to help was strong in us and much nurtured by our teachers.

Very few children had learned to knit before this, so the teacher had a struggle through those sessions. Not all the defaulters were boys by a long shot.

I took great pride in my hand work. My mother had started me on knitting; she was a keen and clever knitter – always with a pattern, she couldn't make it up – but her hand work was beautiful. In school, her teachers used to pay her to embroider their handkerchiefs. That, with her arithmetic skill, had them grieving when she had to leave at fourteen. Years later, she mystified Aussie mums by her determination to see 'a girl' educated.

'She'll only get married,' they cried, 'It'll be wasted.'

'And what if it doesn't last?' she argued. Unwittingly foretelling the future.

We turned out those square patches as fast as we could, hoping that many more were being created all over England. They had perhaps not traveled further than the hospitals, but those now had to deal with the many seriously injured.

The faults in our knitting were hopefully outweighed by our dedication.

The Naughty Corner

I was in the corner, my back to the class and my nose pointed into the join at the meeting of the walls.

I had never been in such a shameful position, and by my own doing.

It was true; I had done it.

This was the fourth year of school, I was eight, I was in Miss Cousins' class, I had been sitting well back in the room and filling in time drawing in the back of my exercise book.

I concentrated hard, I wanted it right. I did not notice anything around me, totally absorbed in my project.

Something made me notice the complete silence in the room. Then sound, a voice. Miss Cousins.

'What do you think you're doing?' The voice was ominous, deep, threatening.

'Drawing, Miss Cousins.'

'I believe I can see that, you horrid girl.'

She snatched up my exercise book, making sure the other children didn't see the disgusting work. They were trying desperately to catch a glimpse.

I half realised my error.

Certain things were not to be drawn. Not at all.

I had been putting all my underdeveloped knowledge fastidiously into a drawing of a lady, full length, full frontal. Side views were too hard for me just yet.

Naked.

That was the problem. Naked. Drawing in class was a punishable offence, but I had carried it further.

My pursuit of skill, my wish for accuracy, was not admired by my teacher, an unmarried lady of middle years, for whom nudity was not a state to be shared – in any form it would seem.

Every morning I read the Daily Mirror.

Every morning (it seemed) Jane, our heroine, lost her clothes altogether, frequently in the presence of Georgy Porgie, a soldier. She could be found coming out of a portable army shower, dropping her towel – perhaps helped on its way by Fritz, her dachshund. She would drape herself sun baking over a mine that had washed up on the beach: a large metal sphere with spikes protruding. The beach itself was cut off by rolls of barbed wire that did nothing to deter Georgy Porgie.

My mother paid no attention to my reading matter. Anyone and everyone could see Jane in all her glory.

Those drawings were beautiful, the line work delicate. I had no hope of doing so well. I knew I needed lots of practice before I could draw like that. If ever. So I practiced.

I sometimes drew Garth, another Daily Mirror hero. He also could be seen in minimal clothing at times. His friend Dawn, whom he met when he somehow traveled in pre-historic times, was more or less half dressed, with one breast exposed in her animal skin top.

None of that seemed improper to me. It was in the paper. The drawing was beautiful.

When, as an adult, I looked back on those cartoon strips, I speculated on the possibility that those cartoons had a purpose.

Was it to remind people of something missing in their lives? It wasn't overtly pornographic. I still think it was more frivolous and great fun.

For years now I have exhibited my art works, featuring my greatest interest: people, the human body and human behaviour.

My wood sculptures of men and women are nude. I have won awards.

Miss Cousins could stand me in the corner, but she could not kill my love.

I could only feel the confusion in the situation on that day in Miss Cousins' class. What was to me beauty was to her a disgrace.

Other cartoons captivated me.

I also followed the adventures of Rupert, the white teddy bear.

Until recently, I have provided a weekly strip cartoon for a newspaper. 'Miffy and Mack,' two little dogs.

The cartoon drawings I saw as a child made a massive impact on the mind of a developing artist.

Doodlebugs

For some time now there had been a new focus for our attention in the Anderson shelter. First they had been called 'buzz bombs,' now were reduced further in dignity to 'doodle-bugs.'

Their presence each night had been declared by a low interrupted murmur under the cloud, a murmur that suddenly stopped dead, silent, ominous.

We learned quickly that the silence announced impending disaster.

Unlike the German bombers, whose position could be located accurately by the drone of their engines, predicting a likely target for the incendiary bombs that followed immediately, these guided missiles with jet engines would silence suddenly, stop, themselves make a whistling sound, and blow up a place ahead of their engine cut-out.

We learned to listen for that cut-out.

'That's overhead. That's Okay, not us.'

Overhead cut-out meant 'safe'. The silent killer had to describe an arc to reach the ground. Someone further on was getting it.

'Missed.'

Events

Many households in London had complied with a Government request to billet those servicemen who had duties based in the city.

Winifred took in two men, known to me as Cyril and Ken; not 'Uncle' as was customary even with unrelated adults.

Cyril was a soldier from the north somewhere and had a wife and children at home. While he certainly seemed to miss them, he didn't make much of Tony and me, but was probably busy and, like most people, tired and worried.

Ken was in the Royal Air Force. He was reserved with us, but kindly. Our mother held him up as some kind of paragon when it came to using bathroom towels,

'Look at Ken's towel. He doesn't leave it covered with grubby marks. You're supposed to wash your hands properly before drying them.'

There was never a hint of any close friendship between either of the two men and our mother.

Ken invited us to the Air Force Christmas party that year. There was a huge decorated Christmas tree with lights and a fairy on top and brightly wrapped gifts with children's names attached. This was amazing. I waited with barely contained excitement for my name to be called:

'Anita Baker!'

I received the precious parcel and carried it away into the gathering of children.

I unwrapped a toy elephant made out of some kind of fake leather, pale grey and hand sewn at the seams.

Tony had a construction set of an army tank. He had to put it together. I still remember the smell of the olive green camouflage paint.

I was quite fond of my elephant, so not pleased when Tony and Grandad fought over it one day, Tony holding her body and Grandad gripping her trunk. The inevitable happened and the trunk was torn from her face.

'These things happen,' said our mother.

She repeated that platitude when my Victorian doll was knocked off a chair by the handle of a broom she was wielding; the doll's eyes which so hypnotised me were shattered. I was learning to hide my feelings by then, but I was truly devastated. When the eyes were replaced, they were not glass. They were not 'real'.

I had a 'baby' doll that was repaired and ruined by an uncle. Her cracked forehead was filled and joined with some dreadful paste. I was not fond of her, but felt the repair to be very ugly. Her face was grotesquely scarred. Later in life I acquired skills to better fix such things. 'Fixing things' properly became important to me.

My mother made me choose the baby doll to bring to Australia later. I had to leave the Victorian doll behind. And Blue Teddy.

Time and again I had to hide my heartbreak. When I am nowadays accused of being 'staid', which I certainly am not, I look back in time to early events that fashioned later behaviour; behaviour designed to conceal untidy, unpopular feelings.

It means so much to me that my daughters and their children still have animal toys that they had as little ones.

Christmas and birthdays must have put pressure on wartime parents.

How to provide atmosphere, food and gifts? Schools did their best, and churches.

Our school put on a Nativity play in which I was mortified to have only a 'bit' part in a group; after all, it was I who had contributed the lantern for the procession and had expected to carry it! Coping with disappointment came hard.

At home we had a Christmas meal put together by the two mothers.

Whiskers the pet rabbit was a main contributor.

Mummy couldn't eat the precious meat. She had scruples not shared by her sister nor, regrettably, by us.

I see now how the war had hardened our hearts. The love I had for the Skinny Pigs in Scotland was a memory.

In the shed out the back where Whiskers lived, Tony and Connie had thrown handfuls of flour at the rabbit. How they could imagine that it was OK to waste flour in that way I don't know, but they had found a large sack of it in the shed and were now 'mighty hunters' in their minds, 'killing for the family meal', using the handfuls of flour as their 'weapons'.

The rabbit found places to hide, but not before I had taken a handful of the flour and thrown it. I was immediately disgusted with myself for that, not too young to know the wrong in it, but had once again tried to 'join in' with other children, an old need of mine, constantly thwarted, often by my own remorse.

We had made decorations for Christmas, first at school, gluing coloured paper strips into links to make long chains to hang across the classrooms. We drew, cut and pasted Christmas cards and made folded envelopes that we posted into a big red letterbox in the main School Hall. These were delivered to our friends in other classes.

At home we made more chains and sat for hours modelling red wax into small flat round pellets which were then pressed onto and around thin dry sticks as leaves and petals for arrangements in vases. That bright red wax may have been sealing wax from the Post Office.

We made the usual newspaper 'spills' for lighting candles. These required great finesse.

The newspaper was torn into strips about one to one-and-a-half inches wide; then the tricky part was to begin the rolling that created the long 'rod' of the spill. You had to get it on the right angle at the top and roll it firmly. I took great pride in this.

The spills were used all year round for various purposes and certainly predated matches.

We had stockings on the mantelpiece on Christmas Eve. I can't remember the presents, but I remember swearing black and blue that I had seen Father Christmas during the night.

A birthday party I had been given stands out in memory for one main aspect. I do remember Mummy making pink blancmange (pronounced 'bloomonge' by us). She somehow magically tipped it out of a fancy metal mould so that it shook deliciously like a magic mountain on a plate.

But another incident was even more memorable. The blancmange was apparently not enough for one little girl, Elsie. Either she was extra hungry or had not been getting any sweets at all at home, for she hunted and found something special for herself under the scullery sink.

She was discovered with a tin of toothpaste, sitting on the floor, eating it. She could only lick it really, because it was a hard, pink, chalky substance pressed into a flat tin marked 'Gibs'.

On another of my birthdays, the 14th November 1940, the city of Coventry had been completely wiped out by German bombing.

• • •

'Harvest Festival' had me staggering to school with an outsized marrow to contribute to a display in the main school hall. Various 'allotments' must have provided the fare. Parks and gardens were divided into plots for the production of food. Britain needed supplies, and food from overseas could not be expected to keep up with the demand. Support ships from Australia and Canada did not always reach their destination. Germany was salting the oceans with U boats.

Nevertheless, the British people did their utmost to create an experience of 'plenty' on special days. Our Harvest Festival celebration, with produce, little treats and singing, worked with the determination of the families to keep morale bolstered, especially for the children.

One morning, a Street Parade came along King Street Hammersmith, with a featured Bull Dog representing Britain – 'The British Bulldog' - and closely resembling Winston Churchill, wearing an Able Seaman's Navy cap. He sat placidly at the front of a jeep, up high at the head of the procession of tanks and military vehicles.

We could line the street, children in front, to watch this extraordinary sight. Visual spectacles were seen occasionally by us on the screen at the Gaumont Theatre, in the newsreels. Photographs were no doubt censored before printing in the daily papers. There was no Television to bombard us daily, so that a parade like this was a great visual treat!

Winston Churchill himself came in person in other London parades. He made it his business to contribute to the lifting of morale in a devastated city. His 'V for Victory' sign with his raised two fingers compared well with Hitler's Nazi salute.

The Queen, Lady Elizabeth Bowes Lyon, and husband King George, also visited the bombed areas, spending time talking to folk who had lost everything in one night. The Royal couple refused to leave England, to reach Canada and safety. Curiously, they felt better when the West Wing of Buckingham Palace was bombed. They said,

'Now we can hold our heads up in the West End'.

Much of the strength in that couple came from Elizabeth.

I had had a brief glimpse of their two daughters, Elizabeth and Margaret on a street corner whilst in Glasgow in 1940. Mummy knew that 'the princesses are going to drive past in a minute'. They sat in the back of a large black rectangular car. We shared waves. Elizabeth must have been fourteen at the time. I was not yet four.

Were the sisters sent to Scotland to avoid the bombing? Did they soon learn as we did, that Scotland was no longer immune?

In between Air Raids and clean up activity, London kept its activities going, refusing to be daunted by attempts to crush the morale of the British by devastating that city.

A determination to '*see them in Hell first*'.

A generation of children ingested that with their school milk.

10

VICTORY

May 8th 1945, Victory in Europe declared.

We must have listened to Winston Churchill's statement and the King's speech on the wireless; these had been advertised beforehand by Stuart Hibbard on the news of 7th May.

But that's not my memory of the event.

I have vivid images of neighbours whom I had never seen, let alone met, hanging out of windows waving anything they had that passed as a flag – pillow slips and tea towels - and yelling out incomprehensible words and songs.

'The Angel' on the corner was blasting open with riotous celebration; the streets chaotic with people in various stages of drunkenness.

'Roll out the barrel. We'll have a barrel of fun!'

'Knees up Mother Brown ... come along dearie let it go!'

We went to a street where some sort of organised activity was taking place and we kids were given lemonade and ice cream by some men in the back of a van. Such organisation as existed was overwhelmed by the random movement of revellers.

In the next days street parties were held in all parts of the country; long tables were created from furniture dragged out of homes and joined by white sheets and tablecloths. Food found its way there by frantic effort. Nothing was too much trouble.

Soon, the more circumspect individuals like Winifred and Anne were discussing with some degree of mixed feelings the return of the men.

Initial elation and ongoing relief were tempered as talk progressed with an awareness of changes they had seen in their husbands already and a sure knowledge of other approaching issues.

Will they be ill? How will they behave?

We have changed. Winifred had taken up smoking. What will Wal think?

How much do they remember of us all, of our lives? Do they still care?

The end of the war with Japan was yet to come.

The Seamanship Manual

The men were not back straight away.

Uncle Bert was still somewhere in southern Europe. Dad's ship had been patrolling the North Sea again, so was handy to Germany. His ship proceeded full speed to Hamburg to be part of the Occupation Force. Dad was required to wear over his Royal Navy uniform, part of a British Army uniform to make him something like a Marine I suppose. On top of his navy tunic and bell bottoms, he had an Army jacket.

Other authors with more authority, have dealt with what horrors the allied forces found in Germany, Poland and Eastern Europe. As a child not yet nine years old, I was not told. Our mother kept the newspapers away from us; away from herself as well.

London was taking my attention! Purple neon street lights appeared along King Street. I had never seen such brilliance. Belisha Beacons turned on at road crossings - round opaque glass balls of light on single, long metal legs.

The elation of the populous in time settled into a realisation of the difficulties of rationing, not easing now; if anything becoming more stringent. Germans had to be fed, clothed, sheltered. The situation of the ordinary German people was desperate.

Wal toured the streets of Hamburg, seeing the deprivation and devastation first hand.

His ration of cigarettes meant little to him as a pipe smoker, but had become currency in the pub where he dropped in for a beer. The proprietor watched him as he admired a model ship in the window. This was a beautiful model of the Victoria and Albert Yacht, about two feet long and a similar height, fully rigged and with every detail perfect. Queen Victoria's husband Albert had been a German prince. Even Hitler had acknowledged England's previous relationship with Germany, declaring a liking of the English. Probably got on well with Neville Chamberlain for a while.

The pub owner approached Wal.

'Excuse me. You like ship? Very beautiful. You have cigarettes?'

Wal turned. He had boxes saved up. Is this an opportunity?

Wal smoked a pipe, but still had his ration of cigarettes. After some negotiating with the advantage very much on his side, Wal carried away the most marvellous trophy of his war, the pub owner no less delighted. Whether he smoked those Craven As himself or used them in turn for currency is unknown.

. . .

Dad had found other treasures in Hamburg.

At a bomb site, apparently the ruins of a Catholic Cathedral, he dug up an alter cloth, purple silk, gold fringing and undamaged. Dad loved beautiful things. He folded it up and debated what to do with it. In his travels he came upon a protestant nunnery of some denomination.

'I know you're not Roman Catholic, Sister, but maybe this is alright for your church?'

'It's all the same God my friend. Thank you so much for your kindness'.

Wal and his shipmates must have acquired a great deal of treasure through exchange of goods, food treats and even money. Much of what they brought home cost them nothing. Would it be regarded as looting, now?

A silver plated fish knife and fork set had been dug up in a garden, marked EPNS but also marked with the Star of David. How many sad trophies of this nature found their way into allied homes? Wal had not dug this set up himself. No doubt it had changed hands more than once before he came upon it. I don't think either he or Win ever noticed the Star of David on it, nor would they have thought of its significance.

I loved the German celluloid doll Dad gave me. I sewed clothes for her as she came naked and a little realistic. She was about nine inches long and beautifully made.

My brother and his friend were attracted to her nakedness, touching her in ways that upset me, tickling her in her private places. I snatched her from them. I hated what they were doing to her. I hated them.

Celluloid Doll never got a name, remaining 'the celluloid doll' for life, traveling to Australia as one of the three toys Mummy allowed me to bring. Blue Teddy, to my ongoing grief, was not allowed to come. Hairless and old, he was judged cruelly as unfit.

. . .

There had been a row over the costume jewellery Dad brought back from Europe.

'You would, wouldn't you! You little pig! I wanted that'.

'He's MY father, not yours!'

I grasped my treasure grimly.

'Nita's right, Connie, she gets first pick'.

Connie would have liked to stomp off, but there were more pretty things left on the table.

I was finally defending myself against the older kids.

Uncle Bert would probably bring things for Connie and Tricia.

I held up the blue cut crystal necklace to the light. Magical! There were other lovely necklaces, but I have no memory of them. Only the blue faceted crystal.

I confess I don't remember what Dad brought home for Tony. He must have brought something, but I was too enchanted by my own gifts to notice.

My mother had gifts. A wonderful set of lipsticks in a box had found its way from Paris. Mum's lipstick technique fascinated me. It was designed to make the lipstick last as long as possible.

First, she gently pressed her forefinger onto the lipstick Then, she carefully marked her top lip with two perfect circular dots either side of the 'cupid's bow'. Then, she transferred the colour to her lower lip by pressing her lips together. All that was needed now was to use her finger to spread the colour to the corners of her mouth.

After the war I found her lipstick set and tried every colour on my lips, quite ruining the business ends of every one. My Mother must have grieved, but I don't remember her giving me a bad time. I wasn't pleased with myself. I had not handled this new 'paint' well at all and I had ruined her present.

The model yacht from the Hamburg pub had been packed meticulously in a box. Dad had his Seamanship Manual with detailed instruction for the rigging of this exact ship. Many,

many hours in the future were spent by him rigging and changing the stringing of that model.

The Seamanship Manual was his before he ever acquired the ship, so it was fortunate that it included the information needed for him to care for it. This book was about nine inches by six, and one and a half inches thick, with a black cover and discoloured, much thumbed pages.

The book was of great interest to me. It held all the instructions a sailor might need. It had all the knots they must learn with line drawings and notes on names. It contained pictures of every nation's flags and black silhouettes of the various ships a crew member must identify at a distance to know which to shell. Dad was a gunner.

It also had naughty cartoons and rhymes – to relieve the tedium of study no doubt. There was Morse Code, Semaphore flag signing and much information that would not be of use to me, but I respected this important book.

My father had brought home another souvenir of his world travel, most likely acquired in Cairo, perhaps Cape Town. Of all the gifts he brought back, this had the most enduring impact on me. I was not yet nine years old but could appreciate the wonder of this object.

It was a carved wooden African warrior, I believe ebony, the dark brown, not black ebony, certainly a short-grained very hard wood, smoothed to a satin finish.

I had never seen or felt anything like him.

He was about twelve inches tall and standing firmly on his long flat feet. The carving was stylised but still realistic; he had all his fingers and toes. He stood firm and straight, holding his spear and animal skin shield, both being nearly his height in length. His head was somewhat elongated, straight up, and his neck had grown longer with the application of many metal rings. I always thought of him as Zulu.

His upper arms were attached to the sides of his body. His right arm was bent at the elbow to travel out at right angles to hold his spear. He had a vertical hole through his fist to accommodate the shaft of the spear. His left forearm was bent against his waist, with a similar hole in the fist to take the thin stick that went from top to bottom of his shield. The shield itself was treated skin, curved slightly across. It was long, with sides cut to long curves that met at top and bottom in sharp angles, not quite points. He had a plain flat fitted loincloth carved close to his body.

Many times in my life I sat and handled, caressed this significant article. It took the same excitement derived from the making of kites and focused it on a lifetime love affair with wood. My right wrist is weak now and my greatest sorrow has been to stop using chisel and mallet, but what a trip this has been! What a love of work I have known!

If only everyone could meet an 'African Warrior' to inspire them thus.

Both the 'Victoria and Albert Yacht' and the African Warrior were left to me in my parents' wills. The Seamanship Manual came with the Yacht.

Ravenscourt Park - 1945

We were headed for Ravenscourt Park with our new kite. Dad had started to build it soon after he came home.

Our house could not have felt much like 'home' to him - so much a place belonging to other people: us. He must have felt a great yawning chasm separating him from the family he was supposed to cherish.

He was too much damaged within himself to have anything to share.

For us, he had somehow transformed from the 'Daddy' who went away six years ago, to 'Dad', this unknown but ever present person in our lives.

We were not used to men.

He must have felt watched.

A kite he was building was seemingly his answer to the awkwardness with his children and the questions arising about his relationship with his very much changed wife.

On board the destroyer in the North Sea, the Mediterranean and the Atlantic, he had used his hands to build, to make things. To heal. Maybe it can work here.

We had watched with fascination. Our mother, now 'Mum', had neither time nor inclination, certainly not the engineering skill, to make a thing like a kite. She was a skilled cook, knitter and dressmaker – with a pattern.

Dad could create without a pattern.

The concept of flight could capture a man of imagination.

We watched closely as those clever fingers obeyed a focused mind.

'Dad, why does it need a tail?' Tony had to ask, breaking the silence.

'That helps control its movement, something like a cat's tail I suppose'.

'Can it have a face like the one you made before the war, Dad? Can we paint a face?'

I hoped.

Maybe I'd be allowed to paint a face.

I remembered the best I could do in Cornwall years ago with my coloured wool and a bit of paper. It had no face.

Still, that 'kite' had meant a lot to me.

'We can paint a face. But have you got paints?'

'Oh, yes! I got a new set of powder paints last Christmas!'

I had my doubts about Father Christmas these days, but none about the benefits of believing in Christmas.

I was still spinning out the life of those powdered paint pots.

'We'll see what a good face you can make then'.

We had a new, marvellous kite and were headed full speed to

Ravenscourt Park to give it a test run. Mum had packed a basket, it was Springtime. Life was perfect.

A plane flew overhead. We had to look. I still have to look.

It was 'ours' of course, though it might have been American still.

Our stomachs settled down.

The grass was green and welcoming, the tiny white English Daisies like light snow over the whole park. Our picnic rug was set near the arches under the railway bridge, the one with the two swings on impossibly long chains right next to us.

We could hardly wait!

'Can we do it now, Dad? Can we fly the kite? Please!'

Now Wal was moving away from the rug with Tony in close pursuit.

'It's good to see them together, Mum'. I said, obliquely refer- ring to the fact that Tony and Dad were usually at odds in one hopeful if sanctimonious remark.

'Yes', she said, not overly convinced.

I ran to catch up.

Dad had to check the wind – not a lot, but enough he said.

He positioned the long tail, with its paper 'bows' tied at intervals.

He had Tony hold the kite while he moved away, running out the long string on its spool till the kite looked like catching the wind.

'Hold it up, Tony. Higher! As high as you can!'

There it was! Our kite! That our Dad had made. That we could fly!

Another plane passed high over our heads, parallel to our kite's flight path. Worrying us less this time.

Flight! We could have it too!

The flying swings underneath the arches, the picnic, the daisies and most of all, our Mum and Dad and our kite to fly.

Paradise.

11

SIX YEARS 1939 - 1945

A generation of children had watched daily as rampant devastation decimated their surroundings, scarred their paths to school
and changed their cities and villages day by day, hour by hour.
Any information they had missed at first hand was spelt out
graphically on the wireless news and in the newsreels at the
movie theatres.

Shop window displays were meagre. Posters had shouted
warnings of what to do, what not to do, what not to say or to
whom. The streets were dark at night except for the display of
searchlights and explosions both distant and close. Anti-aircraft
guns, sirens, explosions and barrage balloons were the norm.

A generation of children had experienced what for them was
no longer unusual.

What had been notable at first was the changed behaviour of
the adults in their world; the absence of fathers and uncles,
sometimes mothers and aunts; the number of house moves, the
newly built shelters.

The holes in the ground had become somewhat too familiar
to notice, unless they permanently removed a necessary entity –
a shop, a school, a loved teacher. That uncle or aunt. Weeds were
growing in the craters.

However, children also observed daily repairs, the small ways of rebuilding, putting back that front door, that window.

Defense, defiance, fury against evil were not the only behaviours visible at every turn.

Tasty meals were created from very little.

Gifts were handmade by men in impossible circumstances.

Art was produced by children.

All these became part of history, a history written during and after the events by both practiced writers and scribblers in diaries.

History painted by brilliant professionals and passionate amateurs.

This is not the space in which to list all the inspired inventors and creators, those spurred on to great heights of achievement by the advent of disaster: the creative scientists and mathematicians.

And the poets - those creators of the most portable and enduring art form, equaled as such only by music and dance.

It is important to note that innovation and invention may occur during war, but it is not war that creates.

War promises only death.

Creativity occurs in the individual mind, nurtured against all odds by the unique human spirit.

Children were being raised by mothers, fathers and the whole of this unique species of the animal kingdom that, above all others, could build, could create to produce or reproduce or to illustrate the world they dreamed of and intended to live in.

Homo Sapiens.

Human beings.

The kite makers.

You want to remind me that our species has the power and sometimes the desire to destroy.

Oh, yes.

Yet here we are and here Hitler isn't.

. . .

You can't go back.

You can recall, with varying degrees of detail, places and events from the past, but with the best will in the world, if you actually revisit the scenes of your treasured memories, you are bound for some disappointments.

The least that might strike you is that those places, buildings, streets, look so much smaller. You, of course, have grown bigger.

Worse: that the working class street where you grew up has become 'gentrified', fashionable. Each cottage in the row has been renovated inside and out; walls removed, en suite bathrooms added, gardens landscaped. I have no wish to see what Holly Road, Chiswick has become.

Even that delightful, grungy café, the hole in the wall that you haunted in Paris as a wandering adult, has gone touristy; the artists have fled to the eleventh *arrondissement.*

I came by accident upon a stylish pack of maps of London 'walks' yesterday. I had not tried to find a modern map of London. I had not wanted my childhood memory of places influenced, the 'photos' in my mind confused. I know the M4 has wiped out much of the area around our wartime home, and had no inclination to examine the evidence.

I found no reference in the 'walking' map, to Ravenscourt Park, and yet, all the way in Australia, I had shared memories recently at a party with a man who was thrilled to reminisce with me. We spoke of the Ravenscourt Park we remembered: the railway arches and the swings, the myriad English daisies. He remembered Ravenscourt School.

'The happiest days of your life' are claimed by some to be their childhood.

How odd it might seem to some if I examine my childhood now, and find that it was those years at 29 Bridge Avenue which were the happiest time of my childhood.

Perhaps some might not count these to be happy: when we were being bombed; when our food was extremely limited and our clothes all hand-me-downs.

Our beloved Daddies and Uncles were absent.

I had nothing with which to compare this at that time. I was at peace with the world. After all, I had my mother, my house, my regular routine, my drawing things and Blue Teddy.

Sad memories of Cornwall faded. Hospitalisation slipped into the past, best forgotten. School was exciting. I adored my teacher, Miss King. I had a boyfriend, Lesley Simmons and another admirer, Johnny Appleyard: we were five at that time. Miss King had to stay behind as I moved up to other classes, but school continued to stimulate the developing mind. Many children had come back from the evacuation houses. Classrooms were full again. We were lucky: our school had not been hit.

The 'Tony and Connie' combination at home was a challenge for me during the war years, but Winifred provided the strong centre that was needed to keep us all safe in both body and spirit.

Our family life and school life progressed steadily within the routine practices of seeking shelter and making adjustments when damage occurred. We had lived; so many did not. The 'Last Post' still wrenches my stomach. I heard the bugle through the schoolroom window, and remembered Uncle Reg. I know now that we were damaged. I must always check planes overhead. I don't like seeing advertising dirigibles (barrage balloons) or searchlights over Melbourne, and object to Air Raid sirens being used in television ads., but at the time we perhaps buried our feelings. We made our own adjustments to the only world we knew.

Our father came home. The beloved 'Daddy' who had gone to war had disappeared; the 'Dad' who came back was a stranger.

The contentment, the comparative happiness of the years in

Hammersmith moved into the past with the arrival home of our father and the inevitable difficulties that ensued when that severely damaged man rejoined the family group. He had no time for Tony and little emotional reserve for Mummy and me.

But that's another story.

EPILOGUE

Wally Baker had come home from the war with a nasty self inflicted wound to his left forearm. His nerves had driven him to scratch his arm from elbow to wrist so badly that the raw flesh reached through to the bone.

Win baker continued to smoke up to the mid nineteen-fifties when a three week bout of flu stopped her. She remained quite thin: six stone seven ounces during the war and not much more after. Wal criticised her for that.

Winifred May lived her life with courage, extraordinary perseverance and dedication to duty. I know no other reasonable argument why she should have held our crippled family together. From 1945 onward it was a project; her project. Perhaps she held to the memory of that smashing young sailor boy who promised her a ring so long ago.

Tony Baker succeeded as a Letterpress Machinist and continued in his alternation of seeking affection and reassurance, and inspiring rejection through his consistent lack of good judgement. He went on to break laws both written and unwritten. He was not loved. But for the great harm he did to others over the years, he could be pitied.

Uncle Bert Page, Auntie Anne, Connie and Tricia lived conservative and comfortable lives in London at 29 Bridge Avenue, Hammersmith for many years, later moving to Dorset and Cornwall. Trish and I still exchange Christmas cards. Connie passed away in January 2018.

From 1949 onward, in Wangaratta and suburban Melbourne, my parents' parties were famous. Somewhat notorious. No standing around just drinking, with the women on one side and the men on the other. We had all the neighbours in. Vic Palmer, another Pom, played his piano accordion all evening; others loaded the pianola when he rested. Dad would have a couple of beers, disappear, and turn up in a grass skirt and perform a hula dance or some other excruciating act. Mum had her one gin and tonic. Mrs Anderson needed to throw up and lost her false teeth down the outside gully trap.

All in all: a jolly good time.

Early notes for 'The Kite Makers'.

Once in a while comes the question: why the attraction to flight?

As humans we're anchored to the ground. Unaided, we can jump, hop, dance and defy gravity for a moment, but we envy the birds, the bats and the flying squirrels.

I have once thought it to be a deep memory of the water-locked phase of our evolution, when we could glide through the oceans, even leap out of the waves and slip again into our supported environment, playing with gravity.

Humans must support their own weight unaided. Also, humans as a species are by nature unable to be complacent, always aspiring to something better, even those with seeming plenty. An echidna only hopes for ants – if indeed it 'hopes' at all. The intelligent elephant desires more than that in care for the group and its young, but has no thought of visits to the stars (as far as I know).

So, as a human being, I dream of flying; literally I dream of flying; does anyone not have that 'flying' dream? To rise above the Earth; to lose the drag of gravity and free myself of the weight of flesh and bones.

As the 747 takes off I enjoy, not only what I am going to, but the joy of what I'm leaving behind.

To sometimes make a kite and imagine. To imagine! To find wool and paper and make a kite in Cornwall. To fly my kite. To go with it up into the sky, shed the weight of insupportable pressures: the damaged and damaging people around me, the tragic and impossible war in London; the wreckage and the rubble; my own helplessness. I can make kites.

It is my observation that humans in the worst circumstances will seek and frequently find a positive path for themselves.

We are the kite makers.

AUTHOR'S NOTE: 2021

I'm asked from time to time if the Corona Virus Pandemic, Covid 19, that has been experienced world wide, is perhaps something like World War Two. Others of my generation and early history are probably hearing this same question.

Apples and Oranges.........We're asked to compare two unlike entities. I can understand why.

During the period of time and with the events tackled by this book, the child I was knew:- people were dying; homes, businesses and social systems destroyed.

We see those parallels today.

However ... the people of WW11 knew: who the enemy was; who and what to fight.

People knew, or believed they knew, the right (next) thing to do, the action to take. To get on with it. To beat this thing. People met in the various ways and places where they had access to each other. They touched, hugged, loved, talked and shared, fed, rescued, nurtured and healed.

My generation has carried what I now know is called, 'Post Traumatic Stress Disorder'.

It is my belief that the young experiencing the doubts, confusions, exclusions and deprivations socially of Covid 19 are right now being injured in a manner quite different from my present day reactions to certain sounds, sights, smells, from my distant past.

An invisible enemy is marking both young and old.

Doubt is corrosive.

We humans have been given, early in our evolution, emotions and hormonal responses to deal with danger. Given an attack by another tribe, the cave dweller will receive a shot of adrenalin from his gland. He rushes out to act! Later, the adrenalin throughout his body is dissipated no matter what the outcome of the conflict.

We cannot physically, immediately attack our current enemy. We must stay home. Stay apart. Watch and wait.

Frustration is a new pandemic. The enemy is within. Despondency, loneliness and fear corrode.

That's not how I remember the spirit of World War Two London.

Thankfully, once again ... new, wondrous 'kites' are being created by indomitable human spirits.

Across the world, scientists are working at speed. Entertainers, writers and visual artists are offering visions of happiness, stimulation, excitement.

Hope has Heavenly wings.

ACKNOWLEDGMENTS

Thank you to the friends who were kind enough to look over 'The Kite Makers' in its formative stages, and to give me their responses. Almost all of them are Australians and not old enough to share these memories themselves. Sylvia Dalton and my publisher Richard Lee, had themselves been in England throughout World War Two.

Many conversations over the years helped me to process what is a wealth of memory and is to most of my early 'readers', unknown.

In the earliest stage, Prodos Marinakis in Melbourne, Australia, listened patiently chapter by chapter of this history, and responded with emotion to each. This was so helpful. Vicki Whiteside, Anita Beckman and Norman Davis are also Melbourne residents and major participants in interminable conversations about 'Life' and all that stuff. The others, in Australia, are: Mary Casper, Sylvia Dalton, Bonnie Gainger, Vivien Markham, Sharon O'Neill, Mike Smyth, Jean Svoboda and Josephine Emery. These were the earliest readers who provided such welcome support and sometimes some necessary bullying when energy lagged. Thank you for the bullying. It worked.

Richard Lee has been publisher and friend to me for over thirty years. His support of my writing has meant very much to me and must not go unacknowledged. We speak to each other in the spirit of English debate. And understand.

RICHARD LEE PUBLISHING

Fiction

Australian Short Stories by Richard Lee

ISBN - 978-0-909431-00-6

Restless: A novel about two young men growing up in Australia
between 1900 and 1936 by Richard Lee (Publication late 2022.)

Memoir

The Kite Makers: Six years of a child's war - Britain 1939-1945 by
Anita Sinclair.

ISBN - 978-0-909431-16-7

Reference

Ducks for Starters: A Practical Guide to

Backyard Duck Keeping by Bruce Wicking

ISBN - 978-0-909431-18-1

Out of Print Titles

Mathematics for Young Children by Helen Western

ISBN - 978-0-909431-01-3

Currajong: For Those Whom Schools Have Failed

by Bruce Wicking

ISBN - 978-0-909431-03-7

Let Them Run a Little: Introduction to Open Approach Learning by
Bruce Wicking

ISBN - 0-90943-1000

The Puppetry Handbook by Anita Sinclair

ISBN - 978-0-909431-04-4

Wordswork by Chris Davidson & Bruce Wicking

ISBN - 978-0-909431-06-8

Sheep Production by Murray Elliott

ISBN - 978-0-909431-07-5

Sweethearts - A novel by Colin Talbot

ISBN - 978-1-875207-02-2

Publisher Contact

Address Rights or Book Production enquiries to:

Richard Lee Publishing, Unit 6, 4 Chapel Street, Maldon 3463
Australia. Contact: countrynotebook@gmail.com

www.ingramcontent.com/pod-product-compliance
Lightning Source LLC
Chambersburg PA
CBHW060752050426
42449CB00008B/1381